D1484021

# THE AUDACITY OF AN AFRICAN GIRL

## By Khuraira Musa

Thank you so much
for your support.

love always

K. Khuraira.

To,

Mama Hauwa and Aunty Zainab: the pillars of selfless love. The world is a better place because of my mothers.

I have the honor of having two mothers, Mama Hauwa, my biological mother who died giving birth to me, and Aunt Zainab, who fought for me and raised me as her own - Without these two women, I would not be the person I am today.

All that I have achieved in life, success, appreciation, and every moment of happiness, are all because of these two incredible women through God's will.

To every woman who died bringing life into the world and lost the joy of motherhood, you are missed dearly by your child and all of your loved ones. Without you, a new life would not have been possible. We love you and will never forget you.

For any woman who has struggled to have a child and has adopted a helpless soul and raised them as her own, know that you have done the world a great kindness. You have opened your heart and endured so much pain and sacrifice to help an innocent child.

This book is dedicated to my mothers and every mother who gave up pieces of herself to love and care for her children.

# Contents

# Prologue

*'Everyone has that moment, I think. The moment when something so momentous happens that it rips your very being into small pieces. And then you have to stop. For a long time, you gather your pieces. And it takes such a very long time not to fit them back together but to assemble them in a new way, not necessarily a better way. More, a way you can live with until you know for certain that this piece should go there and that one there.'*

Kathleen Glasgow

Why did she leave the day I came here? Is there an answer to that question? Did I even ask the right question? Is it possible to have foreknowledge of the events that will unfold in our lives as human beings?

Wrapped in that mystery of life, I came forth. Would I have wished for life if anyone had told me I would ever be accused of her departure? Would I have believed if anyone had told me that the little girl in me would rise from the shreds of poverty to the tapestry of affluence and grandeur? Many decades have passed under the sun since that day. These decades blend sorrow and joy, a fusion of highs and lows, a slate of loss and victory – a grill of bits and pieces that fit into the picture of what I have become.

More than four decades ago, clustered in the genial comfort of my Rugga (Fulani settlement), life began to unfold in the colors and shades destined to be mine. I remember with gleeful joy the freedom of childhood, the innocence of expectations, and the folly of just being children in the kind of background from which I hail. I remember those moments sometimes with a grin on my face. Or a hearty laugh at the life that was once ours. And sometimes, with a call to my childhood friends to reminisce about the sheer joy of our time together.

I remember the nights, lit with a full-blown moon and the abandoned care of childhood, trapped in our nightlife games. I remember the star-lit nights and the fun that came with them. Those moments were priceless; no worries, we just had fun.

I vividly remember the timeless moments shared with friends. The memories linger as I write. Some of those memories are beautiful and unforgettable. Some are not. My childhood days were quite exciting. Running around the open bushes in our formerly peaceful community in Jebbu Bassa didn't give our parents and guardians a heart attack.

Back then, at 11 or 12, having a crush on somebody was pointless, especially for a Fulani girl like me. Around that age, a girl's hand was already being asked for in marriage to someone unknown to her. Unfortunately, this was unpreventable because parents decide on a girl's marital destiny.

*Mallam Umar Gaine and his wife, Aunt Zainab.*

The events of life unfolded before me in layers. I remember Aunt Zainab's voice, the compassion, commitment, and comfort that laced it. I remember her understanding and the responsibility to ensure my life made sense. I remember her husband, Mallam Umar A.K.A. Gaine, a selfless man who made things happen for the family. He would sacrifice anything for the good of his grandchildren and me.

In hindsight, one would conclude that my life would not have reached here if Aunt Zainab and her husband had not allowed me to get a primary school education, a rare privilege for a Fulani girl in those days. Where would I be by now if they had not accepted my request? It's hard to say.

I attempt to reflect on my life in the snippets I have shared so far, penning down the opportunities, the tragedies, and the joys. I reflect on how the bittersweet moments of life shape us into what we become, the choices we make, the people we meet, and the help we get along the way are ingredients of what becomes of our lives in the long haul.

I am humbled by the fortunes and grace I have come into; I am grateful for life, and I am thankful for the battles I have had to fight and how each one has made a significant impact on my life. I hope this narrative serves as an inspiration for any girl who strives for greatness. With a bit of audacity, there is nothing that can stop you. Napoleon Hill is right, *"Whatever the mind can conceive and believe, it can achieve."*

Welcome to the life of Khuraira Musa.

# Chapter 1: Childhood

"Childhood is the best of all the seasons of life, and the longer it lasts with happy memories, the stronger the emotional stability in adulthood."

Venugopal Acharya

## The Orphan's Base

"Birth is an opportunity to transcend. To rise above what we are accustomed to, reach deeper inside ourselves than we are familiar with, and to see not only what we are truly made of but the strength we can access in and through birth."

Marcie Macari

It was the 19th of September 1967, my birth date. I was born in Mariri, in the Lere Local Government Area of Kaduna State. My mother, Hauwa, could not push out her placenta after having me, and the retained placenta made the blood vessels, to which the organ was still attached, bleed on end. Her uterus was unable to close properly to prevent blood loss. Because of these complications, she had to be taken to Our Lady of Apostles Maternity hospital (OLA) in Jos, Plateau State. She was wheeled by bicycle while my infant self was carried in a Calabash.

By the time they reached the roadside in Mista Ali, where they would board a bus going to Our Lady of Apostles, a catholic maternity hospital, my mother had turned, groaning in pain, and then took a look at the little peaceful me.

Just when she was being carried into the bus, she said, "This is what I am blessed with, and I will not be here for her." After that statement, she took her last breath.

The heavy bleeding that had stretched across the time it took to get her to the park at Mista Ali took a heavy toll on her life. She barely made it to the OLA Hospital before the cold, freezing hands of death snatched her away from us. She passed away just a few kilometers away from help. At the same time, I was transported to OLA hospital, where I was observed for a few weeks before being taken to the OLA orphanage at Zawan. According to Islamic beliefs, my mother was buried in Mista Ali.

My mother left the day I came, and my life essentially changed when I came into the world. It would have to be decided for me without the one who carried me in her womb to term. I laid in the swaddle of innocence, a bundle of joy on the one hand and a reminder of profound loss. My father stood by the side of two influential women in his life: one was a baby he had looked forward to receiving, and the other was the lifeless body of his beautiful, charming wife.

One could only imagine the racing thoughts that built up to traffic in his mind as he processed the events that had become a permanent scar, untreatable even with the cream of time. Held up with the support of kith and kin from my late mother's side and his brothers', he processed his grief and joy for the length of time he needed.

My life began at a hospital orphanage that was established by British missionaries. I was there for nine months with other children in the circumstances just like mine; there with people who had a destiny just like mine: robbed of motherhood when it mattered the most. We would grow to hear about the strong ladies who risked their lives to bring us into the world. I write this remembering that, as of this moment, another newborn baby somewhere across the globe has lost its mother, given the high maternal mortality rate worldwide.

The United Nations Population Fund reports that as of 2021, approximately 808 women die every day from preventable causes related to pregnancy and childbirth. Every two minutes, a woman dies, and a poor baby becomes an orphan. At the same time, an estimated 20 or 30 encounter injuries, infections, or disabilities.

I have been there. I understand the plight of the orphans. I remember the stories I was told about the missionaries who nursed us. They did everything possible to ensure we survived our first few months on Earth. They dotted over us with care and love so deep it could fill the void motherhood had left. My father, full of grief, couldn't process how he could handle a newborn daughter, leaving me to be cared for by the missionary nurses.

During my time in the orphanage, my maternal aunt, and my mother's older sister, Aunt Zainab, visited intermittently. And the caretakers at the orphanage helped me in every way possible. They treated me like their own, even though we weren't related. For those nine months, I knew nothing about myself except later what I was told. I was too young to understand myself, much less the world surrounding me.

Unfortunately, my dad and Aunt Zainab never got along. Why? To date, I have no clue. They each had plans for shaping my life and disagreed on almost everything. Each of them thought they knew what was good for me.

Being so close to my mother, she felt it was incumbent on her to be my custodial guardian. However, my dad thought otherwise. As of the time of the battle for where I would wind up, my father hadn't remarried. He couldn't take me to his family. He alone knew why, but he had plans for me.

While I lingered in the orphanage, my father had arranged something for me, unbeknownst to my aunt. One fateful day, she visited as usual, but I was not there. When she asked about my whereabouts, then was told my father had come and taken me away.

Unhappy but helpless, she left wondering what she could do to have me. I wasn't her child. For that alone, she had limits, no matter how bad she wanted me under her roof.

It happened that the day she came was our community's weekly market day. She thus proceeded to the village Kasuwa (market) for her shopping. The market had its spectacular beauty. Women and men from every Settlement around the village came to buy their unique wares. The market was distinctive for obvious reasons, given those times. Here people got to see the newest things available; the day people could buy items of all kinds at subsidized rates; and the happiest day of the week for farmers.

Every child looked forward to the market day with joy and great expectations. It was the day mothers and fathers would buy unique presents for them. It was a beehive of memorable events and a melting pot of socialization for the villagers. At the village market, differences across all divides paled insignificance compared to the general needs of all market-goers.

After arriving at the market, my aunt began searching for my father. She didn't find him in his usual assembly of friends. He had a particular place where he and his friends often assembled to discuss mutual issues of cattle herding and other life events. He was not there. Restless, she kept on searching.

Along her path, eyes roving over every sight in the market, she came to the stall of the famous market caterer, Malama Yelwa. There I was, strapped to the back of the woman who was not akin to us.

"How did you get her?" Aunt Zainab asked after a brief exchange of pleasantries. "Well, her father brought her to me and asked me to take care of her at an agreed price." said the woman. My aunt exploded, "What? Over my dead body! Nobody will raise my beloved sister's daughter while I am still alive!"

Yelwa replied, "Ah! That's just so fine with me.

I don't even want her. She cries all night; Please take her. It's going to be a great relief for me." Gladly, my aunt took me and left as soon as she could. Even at that tender age, I guess my cries gave off signs of the kind of personality I would have. It was as though I was never satisfied until I had what I wanted.

Dad later learned about the event. He was enraged and dilating with rage as though my aunt had thrust a dagger through his heart. It was a brief bloodless family war. He did everything to separate me from her, but my aunt was as determined as he was to have me in her custody.

His reasons for taking me were not compelling for her. "Why would you rather have her in the hands of some strange cook from only God knows what place? Why, Dembo?" she asked, visibly shaking with anger.

"That's the way I want it! She is my daughter, and I know what is best for her!" Dad said matter-of-factly, slightly raising his voice.

The animosity between these two significant figures lingered on for days in the earliest days of my life. Dad grudgingly allowed me to live with Aunt Zainab as the dust settled; that was how they decided on my base. Thank God she had gotten her way.

When Aunt Zainab finally had full custody, she did everything she could to produce breast milk to feed me. She took native mixtures to help her create the milk. With the aid of our native recipe for making native pap or millet porridge (kununkanwa), which she took as often as needed, adequately mixed with the native herbs, she could produce some milk to breastfeed me. Her efforts yielded results, but that was not enough to fulfill me.

I believe her compassion for me drew the attention of one of our neighbors Mallam Ibrahim AKA Mallam Jaeh. He noticed the canopy of love under which Aunt Zainab ensured I bloomed. He saw the commitment that heralded the meticulous care of my aunt for me. He was so moved by all she did that he donated a cow from which she could get some milk to feed me. That timely gift marked the beginning of a rich, healthy, and blessed relationship that would last decades.

What Aunt Zainab did in those early days for me was immeasurable. She was the soft, comforting crib in which my little life landed. She nursed me as if I were her own. She took two years off from selling in the market to thoroughly look after me, making the world heavenly for me. I would say that I owe my success story to God, the largest of all in this world, to Aunty Zainab.

Growing up with her and my cousins in Rugga, a Fulani settlement, was excellent. There are different casts of Fulani from other parts of northern Nigeria – and even the dialects differ within the Fulani community. My father was a Fulani from Sokoto while my mom was a Fulani from Jigawa. My aunt's husband was also a Fulani from Sokoto, but he was not related to my father. According to Wikipedia, there are about 40 million Fulanis worldwide, mostly residing in West Africa, from pastoral-nomadic people or Mbororo, who move around, and the semi-nomadic, who are the town Fulanis. Nigeria is known to be the largest settlement for Fulanis in West Africa.

*The Rugga Settlement.*

The Fulani Rugga in which I grew up had no amenities. We had no electricity, running water, tarred roads, clinics or hospitals, and schools. To get any of those, we had to leave our turf. The houses we had were small straw huts with one door and no windows. Having retired from the sometimes-busy village life, I slept on a straw bed each night. It was a modest but peaceful life.

During Ruma (the rainy season of mold), the weather hit its coldest limit. Nearby in Jos, Plateau State, the cold, freezing climate was unbearable. Often, we had to share our little hut with the rain. Our thatched-roof leaking made us switch places with the areas the rain had dampened within the shed. We watched the rain bubble off our dusty floors as though to say, "It's nice doing business with you."

To keep our humble abode a bit warm, Aunt Zainab often lit a fire in the middle of the hut, which she kept burning throughout the night. I often watched the yellow light rise slowly to lick the firewood until it produced blazing red coals that warmed the hut till sweet sleep closed our eyes. My slight frame would be wrapped in a light blanket that was not thick enough to shield me from the sharp blades of cold. Nonetheless, we bore that life gladly.

It was simple and humble life. We knew nothing better. We were comfortable and peaceful and had no worries wishing for anything more than what we had. It was the life we had, and it was the life we knew. It was our usual.

We lived in straw huts until I was 12. Then, we built a mud house, which was quite an improvement! We were so excited to have a mud house. I was so happy that we had finally upgraded. I can still feel the joy of just writing about it right now. The next improvement was putting some cement on the floor with sharp sand. It was so cool. We even had a hole like a window: we could peep through it to behold the world outside - something I had never experienced in 12 years. That was awesome and a noteworthy milestone.

Later in my life, before leaving for the United States, we built our first modern house with a zinc roof. We then had a bedroom, living room, kitchen, and bathroom - all attached but not like the contemporary self-contained apartments these days. We called that modern in those days. We had reached another higher upgrade.

Within a settlement of ten huts, I had a childhood that was simply out of this world, given the times and our destitute conditions. I loved most of my childhood days, and I never lacked anything. My aunt gave me all the attention in the world.

I was that little shining light she would ensure kept glowing in her life. She didn't want anything to dim my hope or remind me of my loss. She doted over me with care and affection. Simply put, there was nothing in this world that I could not get from Aunt Zainab.

Aunt Zainab accommodated my excesses and supported my unrealistic dreams, given the professional limitations of girls like me. She tilled the soil from which my hopes blossomed into a beautiful garden of fulfilled dreams. She was my angel. She was the one that the Almighty Allah (God) destined to be the bridge

15

between where I was and where I would be. She fought, stood, and spoke up for me when I had no voice. She didn't give up on being in my life even when she knew dad didn't want her anywhere close to me. I am privileged to have emerged from such a courageous lineage. She was a woman whom the ravens of life could not scare. She was a sweet scent of hope in my life, making a princess out of myself. She never defied my wishes, having laid a solid foundation that strengthened the beautiful structure of my life.

My priceless Aunt Zainab -- a shade in the Sahara!

She accommodated my choice of food. I was not the typical Rugga girl who was content with corn or millet paste for food. My aunt, who loved me unconditionally, often got me garri, rice, Irish potatoes, or cassava. That was a rare luxury then. When *semovita* later came along, she made provisions for that as well. My aunt would give me the world if she could afford it.

Back then, the communal bonding was sweet and amicable. The ten huts in our Rugga represented a family unit; some were descendants of Gaine, Aunt Zainab's husband. He had seven sons and two daughters. The other homes belonged to the sons of his late brothers.

He had more than twenty-five grandkids around my age from his children and nephews. I was more like their aunt because of my relationship with Aunt Zainab. Some of her stepsons were almost her age. On the whole, every child was precious to her.

The families shared dinner each evening. Aunt Zainab's delicious dishes were the talk of our *rugga*. They would often mill around our hut to get a scoop of my sweet portion of our assorted delicious dishes; it was heavenly! Though they brought portions of corn or millet paste food (tuwo) from their huts so we could eat together, the taste of Aunt Zainab's cooking was beyond delicious for the kids. We all shared our joys and sorrows. It was a close-knit and very peaceful settlement. Our daily events as children were mainly limited to our community.

She often said, "Every child in this neighborhood is like my child. I remember Aunt Zainab's words of wisdom about children: "Your children are not your children. The children that are yours are the children of others you have treated well."

That has stuck with me over these many memorable years. I learned to care for those that have not my blood relations. From Aunt Zainab, I also heard, "You hate yours, and the world will love it. And you love yours, and the world will hate it." That was her philosophy, and she lived by it. The philosophy she believed in shaped the way she led her life.

My childhood was abundant with unforgettable memories. I relished hide and seek with my mates during the dry season (harmattan). I remember the moonlight tales we looked forward to each night. At the feet of our elders, we learned life lessons as they told us those stories.

Community teamwork and families voluntarily helping one another were the norm then. If one family had a job to be executed, everyone would come around to lend a helping hand. Life was communal; we lived together and met the needs of each family. We had plenty of foods: cassava, guinea corn, maize, Irish potato, and more. Young, muscled, and strong men worked the farms in turns while the women cooked for them. It was colorful and beautiful.

The ten huts were unique in a way that words cannot describe. We bonded very closely. Close to where we had settled were the natives of the land, the Rukuba people of Plateau State. They were primarily non-Muslims, yet our relationship was very cordial and peaceful. The two communities trusted one another and lived peacefully. We helped to cultivate one another's farms.

17

Farmers/Herders' current conflict situation shocks me. Imagine that a Fulani herder can no longer live with the natives of the communities where he has settled to graze his cattle for hundreds of years. I still believe we can go back to that communal life. It was harmonious and tranquil.

## This Teenage Innocence

"It takes courage to grow up and become who you really are."

E. E. Cummings

Hidden in the parchments of life are gemstones. One path, well taken, can lead you to the rest of the world. Given my birth and early life circumstances, I am happy that life is not predictable. If it were, someone like me would have been written off long before the game started.

With the benefit of hindsight, I can say that the people who come into our lives at different stages enrich us in many ways. Some experiences are bitter. Some are sweet. Whatever the taste is, a student of life learns something from everybody. I owed a lot to some of my exposures when I had them.

Celina, my teenage friend, was the one that gave me my first glimpse of affluence. She was the daughter of our local chief in the Rukuba Kingdom. Her father; was a generous and well-mannered man, quite a wonderful gentleman. He had the qualities of a king, ruled fairly, and held the community together.

There was something about Celina, though. People would often say she wouldn't talk to anybody. Well, if she did, she had good reasons. Where I came from, there is a kind of caste system. If you come from poverty, mingling with the wealthy or royals was not expected. The poor are looked down at. Always ask which family you belong to or your tribe. But she was just a quiet and humble young lady.

On the other hand, I am always confident that I can talk to anyone. I felt I could reach anybody, no matter how exalted their position was. My aunt raised me to be audacious. Nothing scares or intimidates me, thanks to the freedom from Aunt Zainab.

Given that courage, I started talking to Celina. She invited me over to her house. My eyes were in disbelief; what was in front of me was the encapsulation of affluence back then: a spacious house with a television set. It felt as though I was in another world.

It was around Christmas time that year. Her older brother, Barrister Ali Aku, the dream of the village maidens, took us in his car to watch the Ten Commandments at the Rukuba barrack's Movie theater. So this is what wealth felt like. I felt like I was walking in someone else's shoes. Who would've thought that a destitute girl like me would get to experience this?

Moments shared with Celina were quite enriching. These short-lived moments cracked open the usually impenetrable door of the rich and favored.

Compared to where she and her family lived, my thatched hut, a mansion in our eyes in those days, was more like a place where human beings could not even attempt to dwell. Even at that, Celina did not, for once, act condescendingly. She treated me with reverence and dignity as a dear friend would to another. Class differences didn't amount to any scornful treatment. All that was between us was a genuine friendship.

Then my other friend, Nafisa, whom I grew up with. She can be attributed to my love of western education. She used to pass by our home each morning, looking clean and calmly beautiful in her school uniform. She had a carriage with her beautiful books that she carried as she walked majestically to school. She left and returned in the late afternoon by the same route.

One day, I dared to ask her where she went every morning. She told me about the school. I was then introduced to the ever-expanding world of western academia. Nafisa decided to sit me down to show and teach me some things in her schoolbooks. That was simply enthralling! Additionally, she knew so much about what she was taught in school.

"You know what, Nafisa, I want to go to this school," I said. "That would be a great idea. You will like the school," she responded.

I wanted to be like Nafisa. She was right about saying I would like the school. I told her I would ask Aunt Zainab about the possibility of allowing me to go. I went through with it. She was hesitant at first. It was so strange for a Fulani, let alone a Fulani girl in those days, to go to school for Western Education. Once I got her consent, given that I was an orphan, a new path began to unfold with the added privilege of being treated well.

She told her husband about my desire to go to school. They were both wrapped around my fingers because of my birth circumstances. I could have anything from them. I could get away with anything in the name of being an orphan.

My uncle didn't hesitate to give his support. He asked about the cost, and he took action once he knew what it would take. He sold one of his rams so I could go. With my aunt and uncle accompanying me, I went to the school and met the pastor who superintended it.

The school was within a church premise. The classes were held under a large tree within the compound. Each time it rained, the pupils would be moved into the church to continue the lessons taught by the pastor.

Unfortunately, the final exams were already being taken. If I didn't attend school at 8, I would have to wait until the following year, when I would be 9, before beginning Primary 1. I wept my heart out. I needed to go. I was miserable, so the pastor took pity on me and decided to test me with the examination. Amazingly, I passed. I made it to Primary Two thanks to Nafisa, who went through the lessons with me before the exams.

I started school in 1975, shortly before Universal Primary Education (UPE) was introduced. I would say that without UPE, I wouldn't have been able to continue my education, knowing that my family was not well-off enough to pay for private education. UPE came in handy. I finished primary education in 1981 at ECWA Primary School, Jebbu Bassa.

Thank God I was a fast learner. Starting from Primary 2, I mostly kept taking the first position in my class until I finished.

My love for the school and impressive academic performance weren't always there. The scariest part of attending school back then was the path that led me to the place. I had to trek kilometers each day. I navigated through the lonely, treacherous rocks to get to school, often alone, especially when the school moved away from the church premises in Kissalow.

I would always have to wake up early, get ready, and then walk. I got soaked on the days it rained, hoping I dried up if the weather was warm. If not, I was wet for hours through my classes. It was tough, but I faced it. We didn't have the money for an umbrella or raincoat. When it rained, what mattered was putting my books in a plastic bag clutched inside my uniform to prevent them from getting soaked.

Worse still, I went sick for months. Constantly ill from malaria. Sometimes, it was so bad that I couldn't make it to school because I would have to be hospitalized. I was not too fond of that period. Missing school for me was unbearable.

I always wanted to maintain my first position in class, but my ill health, at a point, even made it impossible. A major contender in the class, a boy, would often bully me for being frail and skinny and, at the same, taking the first position from him. He finally came first only when I was away because of my ill health. I could not perform well when I returned, but I still secured the second position.

There was always stiff competition between us. The boy sometimes beat me and attacked me on my way home from school when I was alone. He called me names to demean me and make me feel inferior. He used to call me "skinny, bush Fulani girl." When the bullying got worse, my aunt learned about it. She took it up with the school, and they said there was nothing they could do about it since it didn't happen on the school premises. So, I had to endure that boy's torture until we finished school. On the days I had company on my way back home, I was safe. As a result, I often had to wait for my aunt to finish her activities in town so she and I could walk together.

The things I went through were tough. It is astonishing how children nowadays, given the luxury and comfort of high-quality education, think going to school is stressful. Despite how tough it was in my school days, I looked forward to it. I stuck it out. I endured and put up with some very tough moments because I loved school so much.

While in school, my favorite subject was mathematics. I was good with numbers. I can look at a set and remember them the way they were for a long time. I learned so much from using timetables. I always used multiplication tables to calculate whatever I needed to figure. My other favorite subject was history. I'm fascinated by history, which allows me to envision the past. That intrigued me a lot. I love learning from what has happened in the past, whether religion, politics, culture, etc.

History is always a trip for me. Imagined the past, living in that moment, and envisioning what the people in question had gone through. It is something that intrigues me a lot.

Even with movies, I love anything that has to do with history. I love documentaries. I love those intriguing things that keep me guessing what could be going through a maze, compelling me to use my brain to think of what the outcome could be. Mathematics is all about that for me.

As such, my favorite teachers were those in History and Mathematics. I also remember how much I liked my Geography teacher. He always talked about different areas, climates, and people. That endeared me to him because it showed how much was in the world to know and explore.

On the whole, I didn't segregate amongst my teachers, irrespective of what they taught me. I got along with my teachers everywhere I went.

As a teen, I generally learned a lot. I can't thank Aunt Zainab enough, remembering how she planted the earliest seeds of self-reliance and entrepreneurship in me. She allowed me to sell our native Fulani yogurt with millet gruel (Fura da Nono). My friend, Rabi, was my first business partner. She and I went to the barracks to sell the yogurt to the military and police officers.

As a teenager, I detested failure. Rabi was quite clever. Being a couple of years older, the guys wanted to buy her yogurt, not mine. I was pissed off one fateful day because I had not sold my products as the business day ended. She, too, hadn't sold much that day.

On one of the building floors at the barracks was a monkey. I looked in the direction of that monkey and came up with the idea I shared with Rabi. "You know, we can't go back home and say we didn't sell our Fura da Nono today. Worse still, it's raining hard today, and nobody thinks of buying yogurt when the weather is cold. "I suggest we just give this monkey our Fura da Nono, and we can go back home and tell them we sold everything," I said, feeling like I had just given a brilliant idea.

"But they will ask for the money. How will we get the money?" Rabi asked smartly.

"We could say we sold it on credit," I suggested. "But when do we get the money?" She asked again.

"Well, after a while, we could say we got the money, but we lost it," I replied with fear written all over my face. I was afraid of telling lies. I knew that upon getting home, my sweet Aunt Zainab would quiz me to a corner until I confessed the truth.

*Khuraira and Rabi, her friend, selling Fura da Nono (Yogurt and Millet Gruel)*

We got home that evening, shivering in our little bodies to the rhythm of the cold that the rain had brought. How I looked could have suggested to Aunt Zainab that all was not well. She looked straight at me and said: "You better tell me the truth. What did you girls do with your furada nono?" I stood there with my tail between my legs, ready to confess my brilliant but foolish idea.

Rabi, my wise friend, said nothing. She had already asked me all the right questions. I still do not know to date what came over me. Rabi and my aunt just kept looking at me. No one was going to say anything. I had to tell her what had happened.

"Ok," I began, "I will tell you just what we did. I told Rabi that we should give the fura da nono (mix of yogurt and millet gruel) to a monkey we saw at the barracks so that it looks like we sold everything when we come back." The display of that foolishness was way out of the norm. To date, when Rabi and I meet, we laugh and talk about it as though it happened just yesterday. I can still see the image of the monkey and the gratitude on its face.

There were two there, owned by one of the military officers. It was to one of the monkeys that we were ready to serve our investment in fura da nono, only to return home and look like we had made a good sale. It is one of the funniest things I ever did as a teenager.

Of course, Aunt Zainab reprimanded me in her very loving ways. Thank God that didn't happen with my dad. If he were ever going to know about that, I would never dare it. Almighty Dembo would not take rubbish.

Subsequently, Aunt Zainab allowed me to keep selling my yogurt on the weekends. I did so and then made a little profit which I used to braid my hair and buy snacks during the week while in school. She supported my desire early enough when I felt I could make my own money. What a great gift Aunt Zainab was!

However, she was not so supportive of my going out to sell yogurt at the onset. But since I wanted it, she allowed it. That was what Rabi did: she sold yogurt. Being her best friend, I tried to always hang out with her, and the best path was to become a yogurt merchant.

Rabi is the granddaughter of my aunt's husband. She comes from a large family of 11 siblings. We started school together, but she dropped out because our people convinced her that western education would convert her to Christianity.

She is still a close friend, supportive, and always praying for me. She is always funny. Her concern for my life was priceless, especially when I was going through some challenging phases. She encouraged me to be strong. She is an excellent friend who has been there for me.

She and Nafisa are always my go-to people whenever I want to be me, away from being an admired face or a CEO. We talk about the fondest moments of our lives. We remember the crazy little things we did. The fights always had to end for the friendship to go on. Talking to them makes me feel whole. It's a kind of therapy.

I still remember hearty laughs without a care in this world. I remember how my friends meant the world to me. We enjoyed picking wildflowers. I loved going to the river or running after the cows. But the fondest moments came with star-lit nights: Awesome beauty of nature glacé in a radiance beyond the artificial.

*Khuraira and her friends playing hide and seek.*

We couldn't wait to finish dinner and say our last night prayer (Isha) for the day so we could go out and play. We had bonfires so we could run around while playing hide and seek. However, I was not too fond of the rainy season. It rained too much, and the cold, made worse by the straw huts we had for accommodation, was unbearable. It was just too much, especially with the rainwater on the dusty floor, like a strange annoying intruder one could not ward off. Nonetheless, it was our rugga, and rugga was home, and home was all we had.

Aside from hanging out with the kids and doing business on the weekends, I looked forward to the promotional exams at the end of the year. I loved that because my aunt's husband would tell me, "If you get the first position, I will slaughter a cock for you."

That was a good incentive. So, I kept up with my studies and did well enough to win the prize. I always ended up with the first position in my class, and my uncle always kept his promise.

My dad's gift later followed that to me. He gave me my first cow. Every Fulani looks forward to that: The day a father would give

27

them their first cow. It is in the culture of our people. That was simply exhilarating!

On the whole, from school and friendship to community life, I learned a lot. I also hoped that my life would be as great as any great life around me. I fancied everything beautiful and better than I had and hoped I would have that someday.

I luckily finished primary school as one of the best students there. When we sat for secondary school entrance exams, I earned recognition as one of the five best students in my local government. I was very excited about that. After my primary education, I got admission into Government Teachers' College (GTC), Jengre.

The news of my admission was not a good one for my family. Given the Fulani culture, my guardians thought going for more education was not a good omen. How could I be going to secondary school when I was supposed to marry? My family insisted that I was not going to go to secondary school. The next thing on their bucket list for me was marriage, even though I was a teenager. That decision cut short the progress of my education. I couldn't go to GTC.

Child marriages are common in my tribe: young girls are married off as early as fourteen, sometimes to men much older than them, primarily because of economic reasons or customs. Families mostly feel girls are a burden and too expensive to raise, which warrants early marriages. Another reason is the fear of them losing their virginity. This improper act violates the girls' rights. This common practice harms these girls as they lose their childhood. They're susceptible to contracting STDs because, in many cases, the men they are married to have had sexual relations with other women.

Regarding their self-sufficiency, these young girls are forced to forgo secondary-school education; the school-to-industry pipeline meant that attending school was imperative. Without it, your chances of professional success were slim. Domestic violence may ensue in these marriages; these girls are clueless and defenseless. Their husbands feel they can use their inexperience to maltreat or verbally attack them excessively. Unfortunately, some suffer from obstetric fistula disease, which may cause foul-smelling vaginal discharge or passage of stool from the vagina. These girls are deserted, stored away from public viewing, for no fault of theirs.

After being denied the opportunity to attend high school, I enrolled in a community health program at the School of Health Pankshin to appease my family. It was an incredible experience that reignited my passion for helping humanity. I graduated as a community health worker and continued working for the sick, giving them the needed care.

Unfortunately, I couldn't continue being a health worker because I constantly spent my salary buying medicines and other necessities for those who couldn't afford them.

## Teenage Vacations

"Trips and vacations are so much more. These experiences show you what's possible and challenge you to examine the path' you'll take in the future."

Blake Mycoskie

My life as a teen was not limited to the rugga in Jebbu Bassa. During vacations, I was allowed to travel to see my dad, uncles, and cousins. Oh, the joy and fun of leaving for some new place. Those trips away from the rugga were adventurous and memorable.

During one of my vacations, I went to see my cousin in Jos. It was always when she gave birth. Each time she gave birth, I went there and stayed for forty days to help take care of the newborn. She has six kids. I nursed most of them when they were little.

At my cousin's, I did almost all the house chores. Going there always came with mixed feelings: I worked and barely slept. Despite the strenuous work that came with being in her place, I was still happy because I love kids, especially newborns. I eagerly looked forward to her next birth so I could come to take care of the baby.

Typical of my culture, her family was immense. Her husband had another wife. His mother and brother lived there with his own family – a wife and ten kids.

The house was crowded, but there was always laughter: everyone was charming and kind. My cousin's husband was very kind to me while my cousin was very tough, a disciplinarian. That was not good for me. My cousin is a feminine version of dad. Her excessive strictness made forty days look endless, worse than a military drilling session. Unfortunately, Aunt Zainab wouldn't dare get me until forty days had elapsed.

Once I was away, the next visit would be Sallah, the Eid festival. I loved that. In the mood for celebration, my cousin's tight military reins slackened to allow me to have the fun I needed.

*Ardo Yari, Khuraira's Grandfather.*

During some other vacations, I went to my maternal grandfather. Oh my God! Those moments spent at grandpa were the best. He was an Ardo, (the leader of his Fulani tribe where he lived). He had horses and a lot of cows. He had one gorgeous, glittering white horse. The moment I relished the most was being on that horse. It was just so heavenly. Grandpa would always ask his men to give me a ride. That experience is unforgettable. Oh, the bond that glows between a grandfather and his granddaughter is magical!

During the weekly market days, grandpa dressed well in his regal baban Riga (lavish Hausa Men's attire or rope) and royal turban. He was loved and immensely respected by the people. This fulfilling pride came with being the granddaughter of such a revered sage. Being the granddaughter he loved so much made me feel so good.

Now looking back, visiting my grandfather, an Ardo (A Fulani tribal leader), taught me valuable lessons on leadership and how to address communal matters. He was always fair and strict, and his best quality: he despised two-faced people. I vividly remember grandpa giving a speech to one of his sons, whom he was grooming to take over. He said, "Anyone who comes to you privately, planning to tear another, will do worst to you when given a chance." Ever since I can remember, grandpa always advised his sons and others to be fearless and fair, never letting go of the courage to stand with the right.

Unfortunately, on my paternal grandfather's side, not so much can be said. To this day, I don't know enough about him, his qualities, and his personality. 'He passed away before I was born, and growing up, as fleeting thoughts, I sometimes thought about what it would be like to know my paternal grandfather and what lessons I could have possibly acquired from him.

And then I allow myself to think about meeting my grandmothers. How would I have grown up had I been in the company of my maternal or paternal grandmothers? Would I still be close to Aunt Zainab and how would my personality be shaped as I learned things under both my grandmothers' guidance? Alas, there is nothing I can do except occasionally wonder about the what-ifs, because sadly, I couldn't meet my maternal or paternal grandmothers. They had passed on before I was born.

I also visited my maternal uncles during some of my vacations. My mom was the last child in their family. The fact that she died so young made them love her much more, and they poured all that love on me.

Visiting my mother's family was one of the highlights of my vacations. They are very kind and pleasant. One of my aunties, younger than Aunt Zainab, was not fond of me because she felt I had been too spoiled by Aunt Zainab. On the other hand, my maternal uncles couldn't get enough of me! They loved me to the bone, while she couldn't care less about me. However, since my uncles spoiled me badly, I was always dying to see them.

I had a fun cousin on my father's side of the family. I looked forward to going to them so that I could see him. He was charming and married to my older half-sister.

The Fulanis do that kind of intermarriage amongst close relatives. His father and my dad were brothers. Intermarriages in Fulani culture are prevalent, practiced for the fear of diluting the origins or tribe. The Fulanis believed marrying within their people would preserve their culture. But I know this custom might seem strange.

I mean, it was truly bizarre; my cousin is also my sister's husband! But that was my most fun paternal cousin. He liked taking me to the marketplace.

It didn't matter where I went during those times; they had market days on Wednesdays, Fridays, Saturdays, and Sundays. One could go to the one in Saminaka, the other in Lere, and the next in

Jengre. One in the Rukuba Area, Binchin– the best of all. It was the one that dad took me to each time I was with him on vacation. Priceless memories!

My maternal grandfather lived around Saminaka. My paternal relatives, and uncles lived in Lere.

Jebbu Bassa, where I lived, was then a straightforward and modest settlement. My people settled there way before some of the natives lived there. It hurts when someone says, "Oh, you are Fulani; you don't belong here."

My people have been there for hundreds of years! They were living there long before I was born. In those early days, one could count just how many homes were around. Things have changed a lot now.

"If there's a thing I've learned in my life, it's not to be afraid of the responsibility that comes with caring for other people. What we do for love, those things endure. Even if the people you do them for don't."

Cassandra Clare

## The nightmares of an orphan

"When you lose a parent, you realize how vital they are to the foundation of your life. It's impossible to understand what it means until that curtain is pulled. You're an orphan. But then I think that life is remarkable, and the thing that causes the biggest pain can also bring amazing energy."

Neneh Cherry

The pain of losing a mother in Africa is more than the physical separation. It includes being accused as the cause of her death. Growing up with Aunt Zainab was a little challenging for this part of my life.

Her children are the ones I consider my siblings. I have four cousins from Aunt Zainab: three older sisters and one brother. My male cousin, Abubakar, was my best friend. He was everything a sister could want in a brother. He and I were very close. Unfortunately, he died in a fatal car accident.

His death took a part of me with him. I cried almost every day within the first few months; it took me years to recover. He left behind five sons and a daughter. Thanks to Allah (God), they are doing so well now. I am helping them live the vision he had for them. One of them is precisely his carbon copy. Sometimes, I feel like I can see and reach him, but he is no longer within reach of the living, a sad truth. He was my closest friend, so losing him was very tough for me.

I have a cordial relationship with my older female cousins to date. Aunt Zainab told me that I had a half-brother, Haruna, from my late mother, from her previous marriage at a point in my life. The joy of hearing that I had a brother was beyond this world. It was, however, short-lived. As I made plans to look for him wherever he might be, I learned that he had died as a young adult long before hearing about him.

I sought to know if he had a family. I badly wanted to see a trace of him if he had a family. I believed that if there were someone like him, I would see traces of my late mother in that person. Unfortunately, he was also married to a nomad. His family was nomads. There was no news about his family – another dose of pain.

Sometimes, one sits back and wonders why these important people left at the times they did. They left before timeless memories could be written in the memoirs of our evolution. They went in the earliest hours of sunrise. To this end, I have realized that there is a reason for everything in this life that reason itself knows nothing of. There are questions answers cannot satisfy. There are losses nothing can replace. There are pains nothing can assuage. William Shakespeare was right, "Life is a stage." Each plays their role and leaves, no matter how much the audience might like the character.

It brings me memories of my childhood. It had some challenges in the communities in which I lived. I grew up amongst Aunt Zainab's in-laws. The fact that I didn't have a direct blood relationship with them attracted agonizing animosity from some family units.

More than twenty grandchildren were Mallam Gaine's, my aunts husband. Being an orphan, I had privileges, but I also had disadvantages. My aunts husband took special care of me and gave me preferential treatments to cushion the pain of being an orphan.

That did not go down well with the other grandkids. The preferential treatment attracted hatred and envy. They treated me disdainfully and never took me as a part of them. They mocked me.

Even when I had finally left Nigeria, I had to endure those painful heart-piercing chants that reminded me that I was not a part of them each time I visited home. Sad loathing chants flooded my eyes with seas of tears. I called the witch who killed her mother at birth. Constantly told that I was not a part of the family. They told me it was because my father rejected me that he put me in an orphanage.

Each time I visit home, I return to that child who got tormented. The scorn created a deep, gruesome scar of anguish. It hunted me almost all my life. I may be all smiles, joy, and beauty, but that little girl within me longs for a home in which no discrimination trails the scent of her presence. Aunt Zainab would often tell me amidst the tears, "An orphan is God's child. Don't worry because these same people will someday beg you for their livelihood."

The agony dug holes that still ache amid wealth and outstanding accomplishments. Aunt Zainab's words, as though prophetic, have come true. Yet, the pain of always trying to fit in and be accepted at a home that told you are not a part of hurts.

Aunt Zainab often reminded me of how beautiful I am and how kind and loving my mom was. She reminded me of how my mom could have given up more than anything to have a baby as lovely as I am. Like flaming coals of fire and became the glue that held my shredding soul together. I held on to her every encouraging word as a dying patient would to oxygen.

The rejection I had from my aunt's extended family remains the saddest part of my story. One would think that such bitterness and distaste would fade after I experienced some level of success. But in my case, it is unfortunate that it lingers. I was a happy child who was dying for acceptance on the inside. It is the reason I leave no stone unturned to fight for orphans, widows, and the voiceless.

I will do anything possible to give them hope and remind them that they are priceless, simply because they are human beings and not because of anything that has happened to them. There are a million and one folks like me who are vilified for no fault of theirs. Even when against all odds, they rise to clinch enviable heights, and the people they call their own still define them by the painful circumstances that are parts of their story.

It is why I fight for the voiceless. I will spend and be spent for the cause of the voiceless, who find themselves in unfortunate situations for no offense of theirs.

Another incident that readily comes to mind would have to do with my first birth as a teenager. My first husband was my teenage love. My marriage to him did not get the approval of my guardians. They let me have my way. In line with our culture, my guardians arranged a marriage for me. I didn't like the man they had picked for me.

Thanks to Aunt Zainab, I declined the offer and had my way. I was an unusual young Fulani girl, given the time and age when I made that choice. The young man I wanted to marry was not Fulani. That was the most blasphemous thing for a Fulani girl to do. But he was what I wanted for a husband. As a result of my choice, the prearranged marriage had to be dissolved.

The consequence of going against the wishes of my people was a living hell. I was treated like an outcast because of my marital decision, especially because the person I refused to marry was their relative.

Nobody would talk kindly to Aunt Zainab. They blamed her for everything – for the excess freedom she gave me. My aunt and I became the plague, alienated in a place we called our own. We had to bear the scorn, shame, and rejection of my choice.

My refusal to engage in the prearranged marriage strained the relationship between Aunt Zainab and me. After the family of my choice paid back the dowry of the prearranged marriage, I was asked to leave my home, cast out by the ones I cared for the most and from my only home. I was angered because this was completely unnecessary. Why should one be forced to relinquish their interest and unactualize their dreams for a man – especially the one they have no interest in?

To top that, Rabi and two of her sisters turned down their prearranged marriages and married outside their tribe similar to what I did. Despite of Rabi and I's similar violations of marriage costumes I was the only one who was bashed and forced to leave our residence. My head was hit with an unceasing barrage of questions in my mind from why was I being treated differently – was it because I was an orphan? – to if they truly even loved me? The double-standard shredded every ounce of self-confidence I once possessed, and I thought of myself to be lesser than Rabi and her sisters. Coming to terms with that crushed me and made me hate everything about that home.

Although time had passed since the marriage-withdrawal, the teasing and name-calling had followed me. Even after I married my childhood sweetheart, it seemed like there would be no end to this living hell. Whenever I took a stroll through the village, eyes would start to dart towards me, and spiteful glances cast upon me until I was out of view.

I declined to see Aunt Zainab, despite her attempting to come over many times to see me. After her visits, she decided to sit on the apartment's stoop until I saw her. With restraint, I let her in. I stood looking, and afraid of what I would say because I knew I had hurt her. I had never seen someone as solid and hyper-emotional as she was that day. Her eyes were closed-shut like an infectious stye rested on the edge of her eyelid; dried-up streams of tears sat on her cheeks, and her florid face was enough to let me know that I was dearly missed.

She suddenly asked me, "Hurairatu (that's what she calls me when she is serious or disappointed with me), so you will abandon me because of what others did to you?" She was crying, and I quickly knelt and held her legs, asking for her forgiveness. I assured her that nothing in the world could sever our bond. Even though our relationship was mended, my image in the community had yet to change.

After the birth of my first child, my daughter Hadizah, I got ill and needed a blood transfusion. I still remember that pain: so sharp as though a thousand clasped knives were pierced through my heart and stomach. The ripple effect clamped down on my entire being.

I lost a lot of blood. I was in dire need of blood transfusions for my survival and that of my baby. Some of my people had the matching blood group, but they would rather that I lost my life if it all depended on them donating the blood for me to survive. The help I needed from the people I had grown to know as my own would not come along. I was cruelly punished for not following the norms. I was vilified for having an opinion of my own. They practically refused to donate the blood I needed to survive.

Their refusal to save my life was not hidden: since the person I married was my choice and not theirs, my life no longer mattered to them. It was heartless.

Even today, when I think of that hospital, the hurt comes afresh. On my daughter's birthday, I sometimes relive the disappointment. As beautiful as her birth was to me, it is also a painful reminder that I could have lost my life just like my mother lost hers while having me. The only difference with my mom is this: her own was a natural cause, but mine would have just been because some people would not accept my refusal of what they believed was predestined. That was something I could not understand.

I still don't know how someone would be punished for life for making a choice that opposed that of others. Although I do not regret it, my dissentient behavior had bastardized my name in my community, almost revoking my Fulani identity. I was audacious, and bold enough to show defiance and go against cultural norms as a teen. Even though it spurred a circulation of unwarranted vitriol and disdain towards a young girl like me, it created the ideological foundation that would later shape my trajectory in life.

I can understand that if a total stranger, who was not related to me, did not eventually come to donate blood, I would have been long gone. The chapter of my life would have been closed and forgotten. Would my people have been celebrating my death today? Would they be telling their kids about the tragic end of the girl who refused to accept the matrimonial choice of her guardians?

Without the immeasurable help of Aunt Zainab in getting that unknown blood donor, I certainly can't tell what would have become of me. I am not sure I would have survived that period in my life were it not for her. She kept me going, and God had willed me to be despite everything. "Talle, Marayan Allah (Talle– my nickname, meaning the orphan of God) don't be worried. If God wills, you will be fine; all of these people treating you the way they treat you will one day come back even to ask you what they will eat." While I lay on the hospital bed, Aunt Zainab did tell me to remind me of what she had always said about my future.

She did tell me that as often as she thought I needed it. She dosed me in the hope of a brighter future. Then, I looked at her and wondered: Do you know what you are saying? Like, is she for real? Look at me, look at where I am. I wouldn't be able to do anything for anyone.

40

Luckily, I didn't say what I thought of myself aloud. Aunt Zainab always made me feel as though I was better than my condition. It felt like I was going somewhere great, and she was sure about it. "One day, she would say, everything will go away, and these same people will thank me for raising you to believe in yourself."

Now that my sweet and priceless Aunt Zainab is no more, I hardly wish to return to where I grew up. "Going back to what, anyway?" I often wonder if anytime the thought crosses my mind. Sometimes I feel there is no reason to go back there. To reach out to my nephews and other community members, I established a school in the village so my people could access free quality education. Even at that, I have no desire to go there because it brings back painful memories.

It is so painful that I wish folks understood the consequence of telling an orphan or a helpless child that they wouldn't amount to anything. I hope people understand the impact of accusing an innocent orphan that is a wizard or witch and is responsible for the loss of her mother. The thing with negative toxic experiences in childhood is that those painful experiences latch on to the victim's mind for a very long time. Even when victorious and distant from that hurtful past, the victim often crushes under the weight of the pain when they remember it.

Nobody decides as a child what circumstance surrounds their growth and childhood. No matter how successful or accomplished a person becomes, they always remember painful childhood experiences.

I don't know how I would have survived without Aunt Zainab. She encouraged me and helped me build healthy self-esteem to make it through life. She made me feel loved – feel worthy of being alive. She made me understand that the things that happen to me, which I have no control over, are all permitted by Allah (God), and he always has a good plan for me in those things. I wonder from

41

where she did find all those fortifying thoughts. I thank her immensely for always being there when it mattered most in my life.

## Two Strong Men in My Childhood

"Character is not something that you buy; it is not a commodity that can be bartered for; it is not a quality suited for only the rich and famous. Rather, character is built upon the foundational commitment of love, honesty, and compassion for others."

Byron R. Pulsifer

I remember two mighty oaks of a decent character. The presence of these two great men in my life made such a huge impact. One appealed to the softness I needed; the other toughened me to face life with confidence. The balance they brought to my life can never be taken for granted. Let me begin with Mallam Ibrahim Jaeh. It was he who gave my aunt a cow for my sake. That gift's timeliness made it feel like he had given us the world. Aunt Zainab would later tell me how that kind and thoughtful gesture relieved her of the fears that stole her peace about my survival.

The soft-spoken Mallam Jaeh epitomized kindness and absolute compassion. As the Islamic cleric in our rugga, he brought us up in the reverence of Allah (God in Arabic). He taught us, as kids then, how to read the Quran. He also taught us how to perform our daily prayers.

He was a man of very few words but full of staggering wisdom. He was always willing to help others. He was so friendly and understanding. He was the one who imagined for me, in my formative years – a genuine human nobility. He was that spotlight under which my tender heart would practically find the meaning of compassion.

Even after I had grown up, he was always my go-to person for the best and most valuable pieces of advice. His significant role in my life is saved in a treasure gold case of remembrance. To him, I owe my understanding of this truth: The indispensability of human virtue. He always prayed for me and told me the truth about everything we discussed.

In my lowest moments, he would often say, "Talle, (my nickname) don't you worry, you are destined for greatness!" Those heart-lifting words kept me going, especially when the chips were down. The father-mentor figure that Late Jaeh was became the sweet-smelling fragrance that scented my life with enviable charms. It was nice and necessary to have someone like him in my life.

Next to him was my Dad. Talking to him was a hard job. It was not easy to communicate, him being the adamant man he was. That didn't work well with me. There was that girly softness in me that longed for approval and care. I was never going to get that from my father. I grew up with my aunt and her husband. They spoiled me with love and care. No wonder dad's style didn't sit well with me.

As a result, each time I visited Dad, I was dying to leave after a week. He always spoiled me with care by providing everything I wanted, but that softness I needed from a father as a little girl was far-fetched. When I visited with my friends, he always bought us the things girls our age would love. He was a very generous man and was relatively wealthy. He had a lot of cows. At that time, he only had me and my older step-sister, Hadizah. He didn't have a boy. He loved me, but the love was quite challenging because I was not living with him.

Looking back now, I can say that my Dad loved me as much as Mallam Jaeh did, but the fear of spoiling me would not soften him. Being strict man, he would not have a place to hide his head in shame if I did wind up on the wrong side of life due to poor choices common to spoiled brats. His healthy pride wouldn't let him soften me to losing control over me.

*Khuraira and her Dad looking after the cows.*

He thus brought me up as he would do a son who would take over from him. He told me everything I needed to know about his cows. He addressed the family issues and told me what he thought of each. He showed me the record book of his cows and the other assets he had. He always wanted me around for the vaccination and census of the cows. He spoke to me about them as though they were human beings: each cow with its unique features. I guess he thought he might not survive his illness from arthritis.

He possibly concluded that he would not have another child, given his health condition and age. He was constantly on admission due to the disease (chronic arthritis). I was not too fond of those moments he spent in the hospital. That always meant that I had to miss school to care for him.

Our relationship remained intimate to his dying days. He told me I could keep my last name even when I married. It is why I maintain Musa as my last name to date.

My moments with that tough man quietly thickened my skin for the many battles I would face later in my life. His commitment to me as his daughter means more than it did years ago. I can now say that the many challenging drills we go through in life don't seem necessary as we go through them, but the whole picture gets more explicit in the fullness of time. Every piece fits in when it's all said and done.

I lived in Jebbu Bassa, a few kilometers away from Binchin, a community where my Dad had settled, away from his brothers in Mariri, to be closer to me. Each time I visited him, I learned a lot. At the top of the list of lessons was integrity. He taught me to tell the truth even if it would hurt me. He was huge on that. I remember one time he bought some chewing gum. It was called Bazooka. I craved it and couldn't resist the temptation to take a piece without his permission. Dad came back later that day.

No one was at home. My older sister, 20 years older than me, was already married. There was no child at home except me. As he made for his hut, my heart raced as though in a 100 meters dash. Suddenly, he emerged from his hut. I was still lost in my thoughts but pretended I was okay.

"Who took from the chewing gum I bought?" came the question I dreaded hearing the most. "I didn't take it, Bappa (Fulani way of addressing your father)," I replied calmly, being careful my voice was not betraying me. Had I known that my response had just begun the arduous path to learning a hard lesson in integrity?

"Well, I counted each piece of the chewing gum before keeping them here," he began. "The thing about this sweet gum is that anyone who eats it without permission runs into big trouble. Their stomach will swell up until it bursts. I would advise you to confess if you did take it so you can save your own life."

That got to me. The trick or wisdom, I would say, worked magic on the lie I had told earlier. I confessed my crime and received the beating of my life. He ensured that he drove the lesson into my mind in a way I couldn't forget in years to come.

He told me that taking anything, whatever it was, without the owner's permission, was a crime. Denying that one did it when confronted worsened the matter and made it more complicated than it would have been if the guilty were honest.

That event happened during a summer break. He told me that he was not going to buy me anything as I was going back to my aunt, and true to his promise, he went through with it. Oh! I respect that man! Later, he sent the things he would have generally given to me each time I left him after my visit. He told me that a dishonest person is like a plague. Nobody wants to be around such person.

My Dad taught me the importance of hard work; despite suffering from debilitating arthritis, which caused his toes and fingers to be deformed will always perform his daily chores. There were no crutches then; he used some walking sticks to keep up with the daily ritual of checking his cows. He would work with us on whatever task needed attention.

He hired help to assist him in caring for the cows and transport him to the weekly market. He was stern with them but still had a great sense of humor. He was severe and strict at work yet would sit for dinner with them and throw banters as though they were some friends he had not seen in a long time. He treated them like family.

From Dad, I learned to be tough and kind at the same time. To be strict and generous. I am a workaholic, owing to that subconscious lesson I learned from him. He dined and wined with the high and mighty, yet was still reachable and approachable to the most ordinary everyday folks in his community.

He detested beggars to a fault. He was very generous but would never give anything to the one who begged from him. He had a great sense of self-esteem. He was proud of who he was. He had a carriage of dignity and strength that would not be threatened or intimidated by anything or anyone. He had a healthy self-pride for himself and his family. That kind of pride comes with gratitude for who you are and what you have.

Even at that, his humility was skin deep. I learned to be honest, work hard, be humble, and treat everyone with kindness and respect from both my aunt and dad.

My Dad and my aunt were significant assets in my life. His toughness was good for me. He ensured that I didn't get what I wanted each time I did wrong. That way, I learned that a good life should come with merit. People should earn or be worthy of the things they get. A careless attitude was not one Dad could condone.

I loved going to my Dad's place during the holidays because he took me to the market every week. He bought me all kinds of things: wares, fabrics, soft drinks, and the native snacks I craved: bean cakes, peeled sugar cane, and cassava cake. He also shopped heavily for me as I prepared to return to my aunty for school.

The change in food made me look forward to each market day. It was the worst part of the vacation; I would have to painfully bear eating the typical Fulani dishes like danbu, miyankuka (soup made from baobab leaves), and tuwo. They were stuff I wouldn't eat at Aunt Zainab's. I hated miyankuka and dry okra. At my Dad's, I didn't have the choices I had with Aunt Zainab in food. I usually spent three weeks with him and the weekly market day was my best. I could eat every delicious food I wanted, so I could bear the next six days pecking on typical Fulani food.

Dad would often say, "You are just one spoilt brat from a city," shaking his head and hissing in pity for my life.

I always said nothing to that. Our rugga settlement in Jebbu Bassa was a city compared to where he lived. We were surrounded by non-Muslims and were the only Muslims there. The community was mostly made of Christians. In addition, a lot of missionary activities went on there. That environment helped get me exposure.

So, my Dad thought of me as that little city girl always driving him crazy. But he would still treat me as though I grew up with him in the actual rugga settlement.

"Go and remove those ticks on the cows," he would say on some days when we were out to check on the cows. Some of those ticks were at the bottom or on the skin. "Oh, dad," I would grumble out of fear. "You must do it!" he commanded. "The daughter of Dembo cannot be scared! Go and remove the ticks."

Dembo was my Dad's nickname. I had to do it.

There was one particularly mean cow that nobody wanted to remove its ticks. It was defiant and could kick anyone with its legs or poke them with its horns. One fateful day, the Almighty Dembo commanded me to remove some ticks on it. The fear of doing it almost paralyzed my slender frame. If that was with Aunty Zainab, I could have had my way but with Dembo? No way!

I had to remove it. Thankfully, I finished it still standing on my feet, which in my mind had already lost their alignment due to an imagined kick from the mean animal. I was not too fond of that about my vacation with Dad. Furthermore, he made me do a lot of chores that boys mostly did. My Dembo thought of me as a son and trained me as such.

Fast-forward more than five decades later, and I am grateful to him. Almighty Dembo indirectly built me to be tough, resilient, and fearless. I owe him all my stubbornness and doggedness to crush impediments of all kinds. He had no justifiable excuse for a task that needed to be done. That has stuck with me. I now know that nothing can stop me. Through the will of God, I can achieve all I have envisioned, no matter what. I wouldn't say I liked Dad's training and couldn't wait to leave his concentration camp, but I have made tremendous progress today.

Looking back on those moments, I am deeply thankful. Some of the harsh training and drilling, no matter how unkind they sometimes can be. If it doesn't kill you, nothing else will.

In between the relaxing vacation time, I would find myself on some days, early in the morning, after saying our prayers, accompanying Dad to check on his cows. He allowed me to occasionally tag along with his hired herder to the grazing fields. I don't know if the cows in those days were more intelligent than now. I knew they hardly strayed into farms to eat up crops. The herders knew how bad that was. They carefully guided their cows or sheep to ensure they didn't stray into farms to destroy the farmers' hard labor.

Now, I can't help but wonder: why or what changed? The current clashes between cattle herders and farmers break my heart. What happened to our humanity? What happened to our conscience? Back then, people were not judged by what they believed or didn't believe. Humanity was our faith and ethnicity. We were kind to one another because we thought it was in our nature as human beings to do so. We celebrated our festive seasons together, and no religion or faith felt the other was not good enough.

We have not woken up to the change and population explosion right before our eyes. Grazing routes back then have now been taken over by farms. These have been shifted further into the bush, sometimes encroaching grazing routes. In all of these, there is no cause for alarm. We did have peaceful resolutions, so why is it so hard now?

There is no denying that even back then, we had cows that strayed into farms and destroyed crops once in a while. The herder paid whatever the fine was, and everything was settled amicably. Sometimes, the farmers didn't allow the herder to pay because they saw one another like family.

There was never a time when a Fulani man was killed because his cows strayed onto a farm or a Fulani herder carried a gun to kill a farmer because he wouldn't allow him to graze his cattle on his farm. The politicization of everything in our country is now the sword that divides us. Fortunately, more binds us together. Our differences are minimal and can be quickly settled if we choose to understand one another.

I have Fulani family members living in Kebbi, Nasarawa, Plateau, Jigawa, and Sokoto. There is one thing with the Fulani person: He never forgets anything. He has to retaliate if someone does him wrong. The Fulanis that I know would never be the ones to start the issue, but if you attack them without their fault, just know, it will be retaliated. They will get back at you, no matter how long it takes.

I think the culprits creating these ugly events have studied both groups. They are using their strengths and weaknesses to generate unrest between them. I still have my family house in the community where I grew up. The good news is our friendly ways of settling issues have remained the same.

Fifty years later, we are still the same family, and nobody is killing the other over cows running into the other's farm. No Fulani is attacking a farmer because he has sold his land or built something on their land where their cows used to graze. We are our problem. Some wicked elements within our nation are profiteering from these unfortunate clashes.

Our parents raised us to protect one another, not to kill. Whether we like it or not, we will always have differences. It does not necessarily need to even come from outside. It can happen within a family unit. But that does not mean that we should raise arms against one another.

If our humanity must survive, we must find a way of peacefully settling issues. We must learn to understand, even if we disagree. And we must learn to forgive even if it is not our habit to do so.

As life wore on, my great Dad remarried more than a decade after my birth and had a son: my step-brother, Jibrin. He is 15 years younger than me. By the time of his birth, I had married and would leave Plateau for Kaduna. My step-brother and I still keep in touch to date. He is the only one left in my immediate family. My Dad and step-sister have passed away.

Since my father's death, my connection to my paternal relations weakened further, given the not-so-close relationship with them while he was alive.

## Exploring Life

"The best love is the kind that awakens the soul and makes us reach for more; that plants a fire in our hearts and brings peace to our minds."

Noah Calhoun

Love is real. Humanity is priceless. My lovely children, the products of my matrimonial love songs, are priceless gifts. I have had my fair share of giving love and finding it. This lane of my life unfurls with lush petals of sweet memories.

In his groundbreaking book A Tale of Two Cities, Charles Dickens captures my experience. "It was the best of times; it was the worst of times. It was the age of wisdom; it was the age of foolishness. It was the epoch of belief; it was the epoch of incredulity. It was the season of light; it was the season of darkness. It was the spring of hope; it was the winter of despair."

A woman's love life comes strewn with several kinds of experiences. What I thought was love as a teenager was not love when I became an adult.

My marriage to my second husband allowed me to pursue my dreams of living to the fullest. We both worked hard to build a comfortable life for our family. He owned a construction company, while I established a small business importing and selling women's and children's clothing and home décor. I appreciated him for giving me the freedom to start my own business and further my education.

He also gave me an opportunity of a lifetime by allowing me to attend Zamani College to obtain my GCE. After a year at school, I took the Joint Admissions and Matriculations Board (JAMB) entrance test to secure admission to a university. My passion and drive for success empowered me to pass the exam and enroll in Ahmadu Bello University (ABU) Zaira to study Accountancy.

Those were some of the happiest days because I could accomplish something denied. To top it off, I achieved it all within a year. I'm not a woman who wants to rely on a man for everything. Instead, I believe God has gifted me with the intelligence and talent to utilize to better humanity.

My lifestyle allowed me to travel to several countries worldwide, including the United Kingdom, the United States of America, the West Indies, and the Middle East.

My maiden flight was a vacation trip to the UK. I was in the company of a family friend and her two lovely daughters. We took our flight from the Aminu Kano International Airport: it was my first time on a plane! We flew first class: Gorgeous, luxurious, beautiful seats and a fun experience.

I remember one had to pull out the tray in a particular way to eat. Well, you may already guess that at this point, my village people will show up (a joke we say in Nigeria when something terrible or embarrassing happens to a person) to tell the whole world that it was my first time on a plane. I had successfully pulled out the tray, learning from my friend who knew the ins and outs of being on a plane. However, once I tried to readjust it, the tray abruptly snapped. That was so embarrassing.

I was trying to ignore the air hostess to prove to her that I knew what I was doing. How could I have learned that I would embarrass myself? I was so embarrassed to receive help the next time I had to eat. But I was still happy. After all, who would have imagined that Khuraira, a girl from an impoverished, sub-standard rugga settlement, would fly in a plane?

When we landed, I saw things I had never before seen. One particular experience was the escalator. We didn't have it at our airport back home. I watched people step on it, and it moved them down or up, depending on where they were headed. My friend, born in the West Indies but raised in England, behaved with the normalcy of someone in her comfort zone.

Now, first of all, I am scared to death of heights. So, I couldn't imagine myself on that escalator. What if something happened to me from that height? "No way!" I thought. So, I declined the offer.

I found my way around by foot to meet up with them. Alas! We had to use the stairs. I held on to the side rails with my eyes tightly closed for fear of falling. Yet, my friend and her daughters had the time of their lives. A white gentleman noticed my struggle and came to my help. He gently helped me down the stairs, all eyes hooked on me, wondering where I had surfaced from in the world. It was the second most embarrassing experience before I reached my destination in the UK. At the airport, I had proved myself without doubt: behold your Khuraira, from the backwaters of civilization!

We eventually left the airport to meet the Chauffeur waiting to take us to Brighton. My husband and his business partner – my friend's husband – had a small place in Brighton, where they used to spend summer vacation. That was where we lived for a few days before travelling to Barbados to meet my friend's family.

*Barbados's Beach.*

Barbados was a wonderful experience. The only nightmare for me was going to the beach. I am Fulani and also a Muslim. How was I supposed to understand, let alone be comfortable with, dressing in a bikini? In any case, I didn't want to show them that it was not comfortable for me. So, I dressed to go with the flow, but it wasn't my thing.

Going to the beach was everyone's best moment. They went to the beach as often as they wanted. Because I didn't want to be a killjoy, I had to follow as well. I didn't like that about the vacation.

Aside from the beach experience, it was a vacation indeed. We visited other smaller islands. Barbados had many celebrities' homes, including Clint Eastwood, Bob Marley's son, and others. We also saw a castle owned by a sugarcane merchant. It was gorgeous. The exploration of the island was a pretty beautiful experience for me. The coral rift was magnificent.

Another thing about the vacation I didn't like was the constant harassment by Rastafarians, who kept following me. I dreaded that with a passion.

By the time we returned to England, my arm hairs had bristled because of the severe winter-like weather. Naturally accustomed to a tropical climate, I was miserable with the cold. Unfortunately for me, my husband was in Nigeria. I was miserable. To make matters worse, I didn't know how to put a call through, so I could have used the payphone to call him. I had to come up with an idea.

I approached our Chauffeur's wife. Would you please call my husband for me? I want to speak with him privately, I said. "Yes, I can do that," she replied with great relief.

I was specific about my request for the call because I was with my friend each time he called, and I wasn't free to express myself. I couldn't bear telling him in her presence that the weather was too cold and I wanted to return home.

The Chauffeur's wife got through to him that day and excused herself so I could talk with him. After the brief exchange of pleasantries, I said, "Come and get me out of here! I can't take this! It is too cold."

I guess he understood what I was going through very well. A few days after the call, he showed up to hurry his wife back to familiar territory. I was dying to get back to Nigeria. When my husband arrived, we planned a trip to London to go shopping and sightseeing. We took a train to the British capital, another exciting experience for me. It was a beautiful ride, seeing the countryside. I remember my husband holding me to help me descend the stairs when we got to London. Heights paralyze me, and I was so embarrassed

*Harrods, London.*

Worse still, it did seem like everyone's attention was on us. I was probably in my late teenage years then. However, I still enjoyed myself. I was thrilled with the Underground tube and double-decker buses. My husband and I visited Trafalgar Square, Madame Tussauds, some boutiques and stores such as Harrods, Harvey Nichols, Marks and Spencer, Ballys, Russell & Bromley, and Liverpool for African fabrics also other designer stores. I bought myself designer shoes and bags, Silk dresses, Laces, and other items I needed before we finally flew back home.

My second trip to London was to shop for my soon-to-be-born baby. I was almost seven months pregnant during that trip. I remember people advising me to have my baby there. My friends thought I was crazy for not doing it. But, come to think of it, Nigeria was quite beautiful. How could I have imagined the advantage of foreign citizenship for my baby?

In any case, we flew back to the comfort and home I knew. I had my son in Kaduna. Looking back, this only reminds me of how much I love Nigeria. Instead of getting my baby dual citizenship, I would instead he be born there. I didn't see British citizenship as something precious.

My next foreign trip was to Saudi Arabia for Umrah, the Islamic pilgrimage. I have been to Saudi Arabia three times, two for Umrah the lesser Hajj, and the third was for Hajj. The country has beautiful homes, hotels, fashion, jewels, and great food. I had a fantastic experience.

The Arab people's culture is very similar to my Islamic community back home in Nigeria. In Mecca, the holy city, I visited the Ka'aba and prayed. I also went to Madina, where I visited the tomb of Prophet Mohammed (SAW) and had fun shopping.

After my trip to Saudi Arabia was a two-week vacation to New York, USA. It was 1989, and my break came during a severe recession. In every shop I visited, the merchants on Fifth Avenue begged me to buy their products because I was shopping with cash. I stayed at a beautiful boutique hotel, the Warwick Hotel, on 6th Avenue, not too far from 42nd street. I remember the day I went shopping. I walked everywhere as long as my feet could carry me to behold the city's beauty at night. It was 8 pm when I came to some strange sight on the street: a discomforting amount of prostitutes and homeless people.

Before arriving in New York, I've seen the luxuries and grandeur of America through television and the thrilling and liberating experience of being in this grand country. To my surprise, I realized that I was duped, like Nigeria. Despite popular meritocratic beliefs, America also has slums, and your conditions and chances of success differ based on your class. I was baffled -- angry that there were people who had similar living conditions to me as a child who existed in this country of proclaimed greatness and exceptionalism. Where did what I had seen surface from? Fearful, I ran back to my hotel.

I decided to stay within the 5th and 6th Avenues and Madison & Park Avenues for the rest of my stay. I restricted my shopping to those areas. Being a friendly person, I met some African-American ladies with whom I made acquaintances. Together, we went by train to Harlem to explore something new.

I was shocked to see the majority of people in Harlem were blacks (African-Americans) and where my hotel was located were mostly whites (Caucasians). It got me thinking about how divided the city is. Another aspect of America, I didn't know about prior to my visit.

Several others followed those first three trips to other parts of the world. The nine years we had together allowed me to see the world. I traveled at least twice or thrice a year. We did Umrah in Mecca, then spent the summer in the UK. I loved going to London in the summers because many of my friends and their families also visited, and the distance wasn't bad from Nigeria.

A few more trips to the United States and seeing other parts of the country like Southern California made me love the country more than the UK. That was why I decided on the United States when the opportunity for migration came. My marriage to my second husband was bittersweet. It happened very quickly. We dated for less than five months, and we were married. We came from two different worlds. He is well educated, a wealthy man from Kaduna's central city, while I was a poor Rugga Fulani girl from a small village in Jebbu Bassa, Plateau state.

In Northern Nigeria, the rigid caste system determines your path in life. Those born with noble blood or title are held in high regard and have their life paths unobstructed. In contrast, those birthed from lower class like herders or farmers may experience natural or extraneous setbacks restricting them from progressing. Although it can be attributed to the joint immobilization of some social types, class determinism doesn't ultimately slow people's drive to succeed. But your family name takes precedence, as it builds pathways to success and opens naturally-exclusive doors to enriching opportunities. Intersectional identities, specifically being a woman of the lower class, lowers your chance of ascending to the top of the socioeconomic ladder.

Cross-class relationships eventually fail because of sharp differences in lifestyles and personal principles. Marriage doesn't even put you on equal footing: my wealthy second husband would always remind me of my second-class citizenship and even go as far as to say that he rescued me from a life of hardship and poverty. Although his remarks were meant to be slight teases and soft jabs to the ribs, I saw past them as him saying that I was practically a nobody without his ring on my finger. Interactions like this slowly freed me from being fettered by the chains of matrimony. I was tired of only being known to be wedded to this man -- I wanted to be successful on my merit.

My experience of marriage is this: it is not about your lifestyle or good looks. What remains in every marriage when the love is gone is friendship. If there is no friendship, each party accuses the other of being the problem. At least there will always be the desire to let go of the hurt and give a chance to friendship.

My marriage to my late husband, which I had in the United States, was different. We were best friends first. No marriage is perfect. We had our ups and downs; even if we had divorced, I would still be comfortable staying friends with him. It wasn't just about love or changing my setting. It happened naturally. He was my best friend, and then we fell in love and tied the knot. That was different!

Marrying a friend, someone that is there is always the best bet. Friendship carries you through the most turbulent moments of life. I could bear some of the most brutal truths because I was with someone who understood me and was a genuine friend before anything. The friendship sustained us when he and one of our sons faced difficult moments. Engulfed in the whirlwind of uncertainties, a friend will always be there.

I never played the victim when my first two marriages ended. I didn't sit down to feel sorry for myself. I merely believed that Allah (God) almighty had better plans for me and all would be well. I also focused my energy on other things that I could do to improve my life instead of crying or running to people to throw myself a pity party.

I just threw myself into some noble work that preoccupied my mind. That way, I became whole again. I could do things I needed to do without depending on someone. I learned to fend for myself. I don't know if that was a weakness or strength, but it got me through those dark moments in my life and helped me a lot.

# Chapter 3: A New World

*"Our life is composed greatly from dreams, from the unconscious, and they must be brought into connection with action. They must be woven together."*

Anais Nin

## Surviving in a New Land

*"Migration is an expression of the human aspiration for dignity, safety, and a better future. It is part of the social fabric, part of our very makeup as a human family."*

Ban Ki-moon

It was not a dream, but it felt like one. Khuraira would leave Nigeria for America, as she had wished just a few years earlier. It was too good to be true. But it was true. The year was 1992, almost three decades ago.

I was leaving without anything holding me back. I was going to chase the dream I had dreamt. The process of migration was straightforward. Before then, I had been to the US several times. It was not an entirely new experience. But the reason for this trip made it feel different. I wasn't going for a vacation; I was going for more. I was going to the United States to study.

I enrolled at Mt San Antonio College in Southern California. Initially, I wanted to continue with Accountancy, which I was studying at Ahmadu Bello University, Zaria (ABU). Unfortunately, the requirements for university admission, aka SAT, IELTS, and other tests, didn't let me. As a result, I had to start all over.

While in college, I had to find a full-time job to care for myself and my son after I ran out of money and the support from his father also stopped coming. It was also essential to have an income that helped provide for aunt Zainab and my family in Rugga, especially my Aunt Zainab.

I remember visiting a retail store searching for employment in the cosmetics department. I had no prior working experience in this field or any other.

The cosmetics department in the retail store I frequented was breathtaking. It was the first thing I saw upon entering the store. Some lovely ladies patronized it. The department served upscale clients, and that immediately got my attention.

I felt bonded by being surrounded by these seemingly-powerful women, prompting me to walk confidently up to the HR office and ask for a job. Unfortunately, I was often mistaken for a model, given my body shape, size, and age. I remember how the HR team was more interested in the marketability of my looks rather than my desire for a job.

I am not a model, please. I am here looking for a job; I told the lady there. "Which department do you want to work in?" she asked, and I replied to The cosmetics department.

"Do you have any experience in cosmetics?" she asked again. "No, but I am a fast learner, and I want to work there.", I replied.

Given my cultural and religious beliefs, I figured that being a makeup artist would be easier. I needed to work with women, and the cosmetics industry could make that possible for me. I didn't want a job where I would have to deal with men and their lewd gazes.

Unfortunately, my first attempt at a job search didn't yield the expected results. I had to have had some work experience in the cosmetics industry to be considered. Worse still, the vendor or brand I wanted to work for first had to employ me before the retail store could incorporate me into its cosmetics department. The only opening available was for the men's department.

At that time, I didn't have a choice. I had a son and was in school with no means of making an income. There was no support coming from anybody at all. I needed a job to feed us and keep studying as well.

"Okay, fine," I said to the HR lady. But am I allowed to transfer to a cosmetics department later? I asked; she responded, "Fine, but you have to be there for a season and meet your goal."

I asked, what if I meet my goal before the season ends? She explained, "Well, that depends on the vendors' needs. They have to agree to hire you before we can do anything."

I took the job offer available in the men's department. Guess where I was posted? I was stationed at the men's accessory department, where they sold men's underwear, tie, sock, and other men's accessories, which was the very thing I wanted to avoid having the duty of doing. While I worked in that department, my mind wasn't there. My nightmarish experience dealing with male clients still haunts me today.

It wasn't easy asking questions like, "What size of underwear do you wear?" The suit section was adjacent to the accessories unit department; each suit sale came with a commission. The men's department was not an enjoyable place to work, especially as a woman. I remember asking John, the assignment manager, to allow me to sell suits while he made the commissions. That way, I could hit my goal faster, given a good number of sales. I don't know how he worked it out, but he agreed. I remained in the accessories section and could also sell the suits simultaneously.

I didn't like men walking up to me for whatever reason they had or simply having an unnecessary conversation. The only way out of that department was to determine how to meet my goals. That way,

I could move away from the men's department to the cosmetics, where almost all the clients were women. Luckily or unluckily for me, most of the guys who came to the department for the suits will find a way to converse with me. I used that opportunity as much as it came: I sold them the accessories and got them suited. I always made sure there was a pair of socks, underwear, or tie close to the suit to get the complete sale.

After a couple of months, I met my goal before the four-month deadline. I also reminded John of my desire to work in the cosmetics department. Then came an opportunity: another store would open in an area closer to my house and school.

It was a job fair. Interested applicants were allowed to come in for an interview. Big cosmetics companies were present, and vendors were there to interview applicants. Before the day of the interview, I went out to get myself a lovely red suit.

I remember telling some of my coworkers, "I'm sure I will get my cosmetics dream job wearing my beautiful red suit," and then showing them my red outfit.

"You are never going to get that job wearing a RED suit. One of my friends said that wearing a red suit to an interview shows you are opinionated and unruly." Well, that is what they have to deal with because I will wear this red suit to the job interview, I replied.

On the interview day, I put on my red suit and black shoes, put my hair into a French bun, and applied minimal makeup. I didn't put on any foundation or cover-up for the interview, just some mascara and a dash of lip gloss.

I made it to the venue. Luckily for me, the top three cosmetic companies, Lancôme', Estee Lauder, and Clinique, all offered me a job! I chose Lancôme because the executive sold me on its business management training.

Lancôme teaches their beauty advisors how to brand themselves. Yes, you are a beauty advisor, but you are also a business owner. I loved that about them. Despite what my coworkers told me before the interview, I was glad that I got the job.

I was candid with those who interviewed me. I told the interviewers, "I don't have the experience you may need for this job, but I am determined to succeed, and I'm a fast learner. I am passionate and ready to learn."

It turns out they believed me. I kept to those words throughout my stint with them, racing for the best possible skills needed as a beauty advisor with a willingness to learn and a hunger for success.

My entry into the makeup industry traces its roots to my culture and religion, which later snowballed into a passion.

Back in my village, we tried out all kinds of designs with henna on our hands and legs. We experimented with sunflowers and blueberries to get all types of lip and cheek colors. These were the common practices amongst the Fulanis, especially during festive seasons. My people love dressing up.

We also found a good use for the blueberries, crushing them to make lip stains. We would use white clay found on the river banks as the highlighter. For hygiene purposes, we would brush our teeth with ashes from the burnt firewood and use black soap to wash out bodies to prevent body odors. Pregnant women often used black soap to avoid stretch marks. It is the best soap to wash newborn babies with as well. Additionally, we frequently used Shea Butter to keep our skin soft and nourished.

Such ideas came about when we saw the elders in our community doing something similar, and our childhood curiosity prompted us to emulate their innovativeness. It was at this moment that my love for cosmetics sprouted.

I worked with Lancôme while attending college. Taking care of my son, going to school, and working simultaneously was tough. My first year in school was full-time, and later, I did part-time to alleviate the stress of total commitment.

I fought to survive. I was not that person who would go to people to seek assistance. That was something I found challenging to do. That explains why I chose to work full-time and then study part-time. Failure wasn't an option. I had to send my son back to Nigeria after the babysitter I brought ran and left us. My schedule didn't give me room to care for my son as I should. For that reason, in a place like the US, he would wind up in the government's care, being placed with child services. The choice is to risk that or send him back until I'm stable enough to care for him.

Was this the right choice to send my son back to Nigeria? I felt like an incompetent mother who cared about her ambitions rather than looking after her children. I dearly missed my son; there wasn't a moment where he wasn't in my thoughts, and I felt inclined to reconnect with him, even if it meant withdrawing from school and abandoning my dreams as a full-fledged makeup artist.

Before my second marriage, I gave up my first child, Hadizah, to her father's family. Now, sending my son home to his father brings back those hurtful memories of not being there for my daughter when she needed me the most.

I thought something was wrong with me. Nothing felt the same. I wanted to have my son with me here in the US. I remember how I consistently turned down offers that could take me away from him. California was no longer the home it once was for me. I had to leave and move to New York.

Before moving to New York, I met a lady who happened to be a celebrity makeup artist for a talk show host, Jessy Raphael. Like most of my first interactions with Westerners, she asked me if I were a model, which, though these remarks were complimentary and well-intentioned, really annoyed me. I tried hard not to model, but everywhere I went, I got approached and asked if I was a model.

Finally, I took advice from someone who knew a professional modeling agency to be represented. Through Fontaine LA, I got great gigs for infomercials that paid well.

*Khuraira's modelling endeavors.*

"Do you want to do videos?" my agent asked. "Under one condition," I told her. "I am not going for nude, semi-nude, or other demeaning dancing."

So, this idea didn't work out for me. Commercials also didn't work for me because I had a heavy accent. There was no way I could work in LA's modeling industry being too selective. My agent then recommended that I sign up with another agency in NY that does catalog shoots since I'm moving there.

When I arrived, I did as she recommended, and it was going great doing prints and catalogs. Slowly, my modeling career was picking up. Even at that, the cultural and religious beliefs I had been raised with made me feel guilty. Modeling still felt like a violation of my upbringing. Thefact that I was uncomfortable with the profession was something else.

Truthfully, I modeled because I would not be left alone: People thought of me as a model everywhere I went. Even though I had succumbed to the pressure, I made sure to set parameters on what jobs I would do, and my agency respected that.

While modeling in New York, I still didn't forget my dream of working in cosmetics. I went looking for a job. The makeup artist to Sally, now my friend, told me that having worked for Lancôme, I had a chance of really becoming a professional makeup artist. To accomplish that, I needed to work with iconic makeup artists' brands first.

She told me about the ones she knew: Trish McEvoy, Mac, and Bobbi Brown. Embarrassingly, I thought Bobbi Brown was Bobby Brown, the musician, and later found out it wasn't. She also directed me towards ideal places for job hunting on 5th Avenue: Saks Fifth Avenue, Henri Bendel, and Bergdorf Goodman. "Do not go to any other department stores because you will be dealing with the top brands in these three stores," she advised.

I took her recommendations with a folder full of testimonials from my clients, a letter from my former store, and other necessary papers and went off.

*Henri Bendel, a women's fashion and beauty store.*

I took the train for 5th avenue. On arriving, I first made my way to Henri Bendel, a women's boutique store. The boutique store was unequivocally beautiful, but I sensed intensely brutal competitiveness as I stepped towards it. My pupils had dilated as I entered the store, and my mouth widened. Again, the religious and cultural inclination came to the forefront: I wanted to work at Henri Bendel because I would strictly deal with women.

I entered through a beautiful walkthrough with candy stations by the sides, accessories of all kinds, renowned makeup bags, and my beloved cosmetics department. I noticed a gentleman clearing the display areas meticulously as though preparing the walkway for angels to trek through. He put things in their rightful places and ensured they were noticeably glistening.

A swift turn led his eyes to me. He approached and asked, "Hi, are you looking for a job?" I replied, "Yeah, I am looking for a job."

"What department?" he asked further. "Cosmetics," I said.

"My name is Jim, the Cosmetics Director," he revealed, walking me to HR for a brief chat. That job interview turned out to be an eye-opener on what excellence means.

Before that moment in New York, I had only worked in California. The cosmetics industry is all about passion for me. I honestly love what I do. I love being around like-minded individuals dedicated to the art they produce. Working wasn't inconvenient, as I rarely needed to take breaks. I task myself to be the best that I can be.

Regardless of the circumstances, I'm in. I always make sure that my efforts are put into whatever my task. Whether with my children, love life, or professional or charitable work, I give it my all. It was a desirable trait for the employers of Henri Bendel; commitment and steadfastness meant everything to them.

Before getting here, I had a folder full of testimonies from customers and awards (annual and monthly) for being the best of the best. Anybody that doesn't have one of those recommendations does not have a place in Bendel. My store manager in California had written excellent remarks about my work ethic. So, getting the job was a no-brainer.

I still didn't think hiring me would happen that easily. But it did, and it was so divinely aligned in the stars. That same day I visited them, an executive of one of the brands was there. The executive met with me. I was, as usual, honest with her.

"I am a makeup artist," I began. "I am excellent at selling and marketing, but I am not a great makeup artist. I am willing to learn. Lancôme' was more of a skincare brand. One didn't need to be good at makeup to be the top producer. You need to know skin care and what the customer needs for different skin types.

Nonetheless, my experience at Lancôme was necessary for the foundations of beauty. Before recommending a foundation color, powder, blush, or eye shadow, one needs to know the skin type. You wouldn't sell oily makeup to someone that is breaking out. Lancôme offered these excellent basics. Working there also actively taught me how to run my business as a beauty advisor. I took that very seriously. It got me where I am today as a brand owner.

That background also did my interview with Annie, the Trish McEvoy executive at Henri Bendel, a great experience. She told me how much she loved listening to me and how thrilling it would be to work with me. But she couldn't make the final decision until I had met with Geri, the brand owner's right hand. I met Geri and was hired. Right after that, I started working at the counter.

Trish McEvoy, the CEO, was not in New York. She was in California launching her brand at the Nordstrom stores. Trish McEvoy had just taken her brand from her husband's dermatologist's office to retail stores. At that time, they had not been in the business for long. They didn't even have their current fancy packaging. We used to print the product's name with a marker or name maker and stick it on the packages. The Trish McEvoy packaging of then and Trish McEvoy packaging of today are worlds apart.

That's what is so fascinating about life. It is not all about how you started; it is about your vision, hard work, conviction, and passion. Those are the attributes that make great brands and organizations.

Trish had a vision. She knew what she wanted to do. Trish told us about her dream of wanting to make makeup easy and accessible for women. She wanted it to be an excellent experience for her, whoever the client was. Whether it was a soccer mom, a businesswoman, or a female executive, Trish McEvoy tried to make it easy to travel with their makeup by creating a makeup planner.

Having made it on the staff,Iwasn't a perfect makeup artist, but I could sell. I was communicative, indiscriminate, and a great listener. You can only effectively sell something to a client when you are able to listen to their concerns.

Trish McEvoy's company agreed to train me in makeup artistry. It was great working at Henri Bendel, one of the most prestigious beauty boutiques in New York; America's most prominent socialites, the wives of Donald Trump, and many other people of the upper class and celebrities all shopped there. Given my background, being privileged to work in such a place was enough for me. I was one of the highly-paid makeup artists. I poured my heart and soul into it and was grateful to be there.

On the other hand, Trish McEvoy saw something in me that I hadn't seen myself. She had a habit of coming upstairs to a balcony overlooking the counter, where she could see everyone working in the cosmetics department. Trish did it in a way that was hard to notice and discreet. Unknown to the employees at work, she would climb upstairs to supervise each artist's performance below.

I was working at Trish McEvoy for a few months, but I didn't know who Trish was. She hadn't been there when Geri hired me, if you recall. I didn't know that Trish knew me, noticed my work ethic, and monitored me for two months. She observed how I interacted with clients and related with other artists in the department.

One fateful day, the account executive, Annie notified me that Trish wanted to see me. That would be my first time meeting her. I was nervous, though I knew I had been selling well. I was a top producer, but on hearing the boss wanted to see me, I asked the same questions any typical employee would ask. "Did I do something wrong? Am I producing enough? Am I dressed well?"

Trish was quite particular about how her artists should dress. We all had to have manicured nails. We often get gift certificates for our birthdays for J Sisters to do our nails and facials. They were the manicurists behind Victoria's Secret models, also known for Brazilian bikini waxing. That was how She wanted her makeup artists to look good: perfect hair, skin, nails, and clothing. She wanted us to fit into an A-class of makeup artists. I wondered where I had erred. The fact that I was one of two black makeup artists in the company at that time petrified me even more. Many things crossed my mind before the meeting.

But then I finally met her. "Oh! You are so beautiful!" Trish exclaimed when I entered her office. "You look like Iman!" Iman was a supermodel at that time. That said, our conversation continued.

"Congratulations on being a part of the Trish McEvoy Family!" She said. "I have been observing you. You are doing great. I want to promote you. I want you to train my makeup artists regionally in the area of sales." I was happy and emotional at the same time. That wasn't what I had expected.

It is how I started climbing up the ladder. Trish told me about how well I did with people. She wanted me to train her makeup artists on how to interact with clients. She also wanted me to help them become great producers to help boost their sales. I never imagined being given this opportunity would open more doors. Little did I know it was the beginning of many great things to come my way. That first promotion from working behind the counter to a trainer in sales was way out of my expectations.

My first training was for new hires and those that needed it around New York, New Jersey, and Connecticut, states that made up the heavily commercialized Tri-State Area. I began training other makeup artists from different stores to scale their numbers and educating them on how to strategize on doing makeup applications or lessons—setting their weekly, monthly, and annual goals. I did that for about four months, and things were going great. Trish had booked me to be with her at one of her all-star events, where she brought out her A-list makeup artists.

One thing comes to mind about that time in New York. I had relocated from California to New York without being familiar with the area. I risked it and hired a private taxi to take me to the event location in New Jersey because it was the right thing to do back then. I lived in Queens. Uber was unavailable then, and riding the bus to the venue would only waste time.

However, my cab driver was unfamiliar with the route and got lost. Hence, I arrived at the venue two hours later than the time I was supposed to. At that time, I thought of New Jersey as another country. To my dismay, I was hours late to my first regional event, in which the CEO was in attendance. Despite my tardiness, Trish believed in my abilities.

Anyway, I apologized profusely. Trish later heard that I had paid seventy dollars to hire a private cab man without expecting the company to pay me back. That proved to her that I was serious about the job. I was committed to Trish McEvoy, and I could do anything to prove it.

Trish's events were always well organized. She usually went out to the company's events with twelve of her makeup artists and three executives. There were always about four of us from New York, the national base, and others from her regional branches. I was relatively new to the Trish excellence culture. Each time I did makeup before I started traveling with Trish, I used to avoid using a specific eye shadow palette because I wasn't comfortable with the colors. I was not good with them and was scared to ask for help from my more-experienced coworkers and higher-ups.

At our regional event in New Jersey, fifty customers came in to meet with Trish and her team. Trish also did makeup, but during

74

the regional and national events, she only talked to customers and inquired about their lifestyle so she could recommend colors, then moved on. My first customer at the New Jersey event was a brunette. I consulted with Trish, who suggested the eye colors I had avoided for months. I was in a deep mess. First of all, her body language said she was not happy with me for coming late to a huge event. In addition to that, I was going to mess up her client. At that point, I was overwhelmed and wanted to leave the event altogether.

When I was done with the makeup, I could judge for myself. The job was terrible. The client's face said it all. Trish's immediate assistant saw the makeup and came to my rescue. He fixed the mess I had created. The woman eventually bought some beauty items, but it wasn't a good sale.

After that miserable day for me, Trish took all of us to dinner at a fancy restaurant. She always lodges us in one of the most beautiful hotels whenever we travel. That was one sweet thing about her. She made sure we were all comfortable wherever we went. The company would excellently plan our trips. The limousine service picks us up from the airport to our hotel and venue for the events.

Trish cared a great deal about her employees. Her treatments were first-class. After the event, I was the first person she picked out during our evaluation session. "Queen Iman here, was two hours late, and did you guys see her makeup job? Oh my god! Girl, if I am going to grade you, you are a D makeup artist." Those were the exact words she used.

"This is what we're going do," she continued. "When you return, you'll work with Alfonzo, Carlos, Richie, and Pam." I agreed. She didn't tongue-lash me. She told me what I needed to hear now.

Plus, the individuals she had mentioned were top makeup artists. "Our next event is at Louis Boston, high-end clothing and beauty store in Boston. You better not miss your flight and make sure you know what you are doing because we can't afford to be behind on time," she warned.

We returned to base after that. But the folks Trish had asked to train me were indifferent and didn't care about execution. I took it upon myself to make a difference. I was not going to have an excuse the next time. I had thirty days before our next event in Boston. I needed to prove to Trish that I was not a D-grade makeup artist. I practiced and practiced until I finally got it down.

We went to the event in Boston. I exceeded expectations.

I was top in sales, and customers were happy, and I had added to my ability to sell the ability to do makeup.

That evening, Trish said at our dinner, "If each of my artists will take criticism as Khuraira did, my company will be out of this world. It is what it should be: taking that criticism and using it to show that you are not what people think of you."

She was so happy. She was proud of me, and I was so proud of myself. Thanks to Aunt Zainab and my Dad for training me to have that thick skin. I have never been afraid of critics or anything alike. Sometimes it feels like I am too stubborn. No, it's because I know what I want. I know those good things do not come with ease. You have to work for them. There is no shortcut to greatness. If you're going to be good at something, you have to give it your all, which I did.

I had proved to Trish that I was not a failure. Now, I needed to prove that I would rise three times above whatever she thought I was. And grow, I did. After Boston, I got promoted to a national makeup artist. In less than six months, I had gone from being a behind-the-counter makeup artist to a regional makeupartist, to a national makeup artist, traveling all over the country, teaching makeup artists how to do their thing and boost sales. At the same time, I met with clients, promoting our new products and other things.

I wound up spending four years with Trish. I traveled all over the US, Canada, and the UK, training makeup artists and launching new products. By my fourth year, I had plateaued professionally. I was making a lot of money hourly, but I needed to do something about my career: make more money or switch to management. I wanted to maintain my National Makeup Artist status.

At about that time, an opportunity with a new cosmetics brand, Laura Mercier, came along. They were hunting for the best of the best to join their national team. Trish had been good to me. With Trish McEvoy, I hit the peak of my career in the makeup industry. She permitted me to go on a vacation to spend quality time with my kids in Nigeria. Those vacations were without pay, but they gave me my benefits, which were quite good. Trish mentored me. She pushed me as hard as I needed to grow. With all that I had gotten from her, I couldn't just leave immediately. It took me a while before I finally left.

Janet Gurwitch, former Vice President of Neiman Marcus, a high-end department store for the socialites and wealthy Americans where using Black American Express cards is a norm, founded Laura Mercier cosmetics. Laura Mercier, a French-born celebrity makeup artist, is the brain behind the Brand. She created all the products.

After the brand launched at Henri Bendel, they went all out to find the best makeup artists in New York and beyond to join their national team. They approached me, given the profile I had built. But I couldn't give them a response without talking to my boss, so I went to Trish.

"Trish…" I began. "Laura Mercier has made me an offer. I don't want to go, but if you can't match their pay, then if you don't mind, I want to take that opportunity and try them out."

"My darling," replied Trish in that sweet voice of hers. "Right now, you are at the top in what you are making. If I add any more to it, you'll put in way more than what you are giving, which will stress you out. I would love to keep you, but you got my blessings if you get an opportunity that will pay you more. Just know that you can always come home if it doesn't work out because this is home for you." After that brief conversation, she gave me the hug of a lifetime. "Thank you so much!" I said, "I love you so much."

I accepted the offer with Laura Mercier doing almost the same thing I did at Trish McEvoy. Here, I was given an opportunity in product development. That was quite exciting because I could come up with a color as a makeup artist for the brand, which was fascinating.

While I was still with Trish McEvoy, I was in San Francisco at an affluent Indian community for a National makeup event a few months before leaving Trish McEvoy Cosmetics. Being the perfectionist I am, I was frustrated with not finding the right color mix of concealers to neutralize the dark circles on my clients' faces. Women of color naturally have dark circles. I knew orange neutralizes blue. If you want to brighten it, put in an orange pigment.

So, I decided to use red-orange lipstick as the neutralizer before the concealer. I used a concealer brush, warmed it up, and used it on the dark area before putting in the matching concealer, voila: everything was neutral. That idea sold massively at the event. We sold out the lipstick.

I started doing that on every woman with dark circles. It became my secret tip, but I wanted it as a primer instead of using lipstick.

I was with Laura Mercier for three and a half years. We always had annual retreats, during which national and international makeup artists met with Janet and the rest of the corporate team in

Houston. Every national makeup artist brought their pet projects to be pitched for the upcoming product to be launched.

Our reflections revolved around things that were out there. What is needed by the consumer? I pitched the orange lipstick story as an idea for a dark circle primer to neutralize dark circles whenever we went for the retreat. I got frustrated that my concept of the dark circle primer didn't get picked, but they allowed me to create a tinted moisturizer for dark skin; Walnut is one of their top-selling tinted moisturizers today. I came up with the color they lacked in the dark skin colors segment.

Another opportunity that came my way was working with Trista and Ryan during their courtship on The Bachelorette. I did their makeup for all their shoots in New York and Saint Martin Island for their bachelorette party. I was responsible for the trial makeup for the weddingas well.

Laura Mercier was the makeup brand picked for the show. As a national makeup artist and one of Laura's assistants, I'm usually among those who work on some high-profile makeup on her behalf. I was supposed to be present at the wedding held at The Lodge Luxury Resort in Rancho Mirage, California, televised and watched by over 26 million viewers. Unfortunately, a week before my flight to the wedding, I got a blood clot and was hospitalized. I was in a hospital bed being treated and watching what would have been the highlight of my career as a makeup artist on TV. Trista is now happily married with two beautiful children. Both are madly in love with each other and exceptionally humble people. Overall, working with them was a blast.

I followed up on every due process until I secured a place in the makeup industry. In that industry, my life experienced a whole new level of change.

"You will be defined not just by what you achieve but by how you survive."

Sheryl Sandberg

*The making of the Khuraira brand.*

After acquiring success from working under other well-known cosmetics brands, it was time to begin my path into the makeup industry.

The honing of my skills started from behind the beauty counter. Later, traveling the world, educating women and makeup artists in the art of makeup. The countless beauty seminars allowed me to hear the beauty concerns of many women. Some women badly needed professional makeup boutiques they could go to, while others had difficulties finding the right makeup for themselves, especially women of color.

Three and a half years after working with Laura Mercier, I married again. I gave birth to my twin boys, Kamil and Jamil. I couldn't keep up with the tight traveling schedule at work. I used to travel every Thursday and return on Sunday, almost every week of the month, except for summertime when I had to visit family in Nigeria. It was tough. I had to step down from being a national makeup artist to becoming a regional trainer to be able to spend time with my kids. That was a great relief for my husband, who needed me home.

Given the changes that marriage brought to my life, my engagement with the brand I had worked for kept dwindling until I finally felt it was time for Khuraira to resign from Laura Mercier. I used the beauty concerns of many women I met during my travels to start a beauty service business closer to home in Englewood, NJ. The women in Bergen County were the perfect niche for what I wanted to do.

They were already clients of Saks Fifth, Henri Bendel, and Bergdorf Goodman, where I have been stationed for seven years. Based on that niche, in 2004, I started a beauty service business, teaching my clients how to use their makeup and helping them shop for the right colors while at the same time doing the makeup for their special events. That was easy to begin with, given the experiences of doing makeup. Each time I did it, the remarks tilted towards a demand for more. Some wished I could teach them, and others wished I could do their weddings, their daughter's weddings, bridal parties for their son's wedding, Bar/Bat mitzvahs, proms, etc. Some even wished they could hire me as their beauty guru.

I had just spent a year doing that when my following grew, thanks partly to a 2005 editorial about me and my technique of creating a flawless face using airbrush makeup. It was huge! I was getting many clients. I got so busy that I left the salon and opened a storefront in 2006.

That was a great move. Two years in, my customers no longer wanted me to recommend other brands. They wanted me to create my brand since I was good at understanding pigments and undertones. They wanted my products. I was initially nervous, but I also knew it could be a good idea. I discussed it with my husband. Being the marketing genius that he was, his response was thought-provoking.

"Well, if you will do it, what will make you different? You have big brands like Bobbi Brown, Trish McEvoy, and others as competitors. How can you compete with them or get their clients to come to you instead?" he asked.

We concluded that I could begin with a product that could shake the industry and get me ahead. And so, my late husband helped lay the foundation of Khuraira Cosmetics. He was there when it mattered the most. I sorted out structural and systemic issues in running a business with him, then moved forward with creating the products. I went to a company that produced products for the most prominent brands.

*Khuraira's first five cosmetic inventions.*

I shared my idea of the lipstick story with them, which also gave birth to the concept of the dark circle primer. I also shared the vision for peptides with vitamin E incorporated in the face primer, a dark circle primer, concealers, and foundations. I added a fifth product called "Invisible Powder," used for a touch-up to complete the look of the flawless face. The face primer, foundation, and concealer moisturize and plump the skin, giving it a perfect flawless look. They were hyped about the idea and promised they could make those products for me. I went back and forth for a year and a half to develop the products.

We added lipsticks and lip glosses which my eldest son, Salim, helped name. I got the support of friends in the industry as well. I got the word around about what I was building, and slowly but surely, things began to pick up.

*Khuraira with her team at a trade show.*

I eventually pulled together a team and launched Khuraira Cosmetics around 2008. We did well that year. In 2009, we did even better. The business improved as we tried our best to build a brand that could withstand time. We maintained that great performance throughout 2010 and 2011.

As we continued to make progress, 2012 and 2013 became our best years ever. The brand came alive, and people learned about it nationally and internationally. It gained popularity in the US and was featured in many beauty magazines, blogs, and shopping networks. We were performing well in France, Nigeria, and Cameroon as well. My daughter, Hadizah, helped launch the brand in Nigeria and Cameroon while I oversaw the US and French markets. The boys, Salim, Kamil, Jamil, and Hanif, helped with labeling and packing whenever we got large orders. Everyone in the family played a role that tremendously helped with the cost of running it.

*Different roles of Khuraira's family*

Our brand got lots of attention from the media after our dark circle primer was published on InStyle -Wedding and Essence as a must-have product for stubborn dark circles.

Around that time, I was invited to do make up for a celebrity wedding. I learned that many celebrities would attend the event from the bride-to-be, Erika Jones, whose wedding makeup I was contracted to do. The groom, Kevin Liles, an executive music producer, was friends with Oprah Winfrey and Gayle King. Therefore, she advised me to package some Khuraira products, including my invisible powder, and present it to Oprah at the wedding. It was a great opportunity, so I did just as my client had suggested.

However, Oprah couldn't make it to the wedding as she was in South Africa for another function. Fortunately, her best friend Gayle King was at the wedding. When I gave her the products I had packed for both her and Oprah, she was happy and promised she would provide Oprah with her package when she returned in September.

I never got any feedback from either of them, which made me sad, thinking that I didn't have a good enough product for Oprah. I thought she didn't like it since I didn't hear from them. Her show was also coming to an end. The Oprah Show Finale aired for two days in 2011.

On the morning of the show's last day, I received a call from a 312-area code number. On the other side of the line was a gentleman who said he had issues ordering our invisible finishing powder online. He told me he was a TV producer and needed it for a TV show. I told him we had it in stock, but I could take his order over the phone if he still had issues.

A few minutes later, I got another call with a 305-area code, Miami's. This time, it was a young lady asking about the same powder. She also urgently needed it for a show. She told me she was an intern working for a TV show. The lady sounded a little confused and told me she would call me back. As soon as she hung up, a client called me for an appointment, and I told her about the previous calls. I said it might have been the Oprah people, and we laughed it off.

My assistant and I watched the Oprah finale with a few clients at our boutique. Right after the show ended, everyone left while I sat there staring at the credits, thinking in my head that this was it. I didn't make it to Oprah and started wondering whether she didn't get her package or got it, but the products were not good enough.

My thoughts were interrupted by a phone call. When I went to pick it up, I said aloud, "Now the Oprah people are calling." To my astonishment, the caller ID read Harpo Production. I was shocked and excited but wanted to act professionally.

"Hello, thanks for calling Khuraira Cosmetics," I acknowledged the call, and a lady pleasantly answered. "Hi, we need your invisible powder shipped to us as soon as possible. Our producers have been trying to order it since morning. Do you have it in stock?"

"Yes," I answered excitedly.

Then she said, "Please, we need the Invisible powder to be overnighted because we are going outside the country for a show."

I said, "No problem," without hesitation. The lady then went on to tell me that the product was meant for a huge production company. Thus, we should not mess up the shipment. She did not know I had already seen the name but was trying to be cool. Then she suddenly asked my name. Although I initially wanted to conceal my identity, I figured I was too excited to do so. Eventually, I told her my name, and she screamed.

"Well, I'm calling from Harpo Production," she told me.

"Oprah loves your invisible powder because it works well when used for touch-ups," she added. It was a definitive moment in my blossoming makeup career. Although I was initially dismayed because I thought Oprah was dissatisfied with my makeup products, this call affirmed my existence in the hyper-competitive makeup industry and raised my confidence more than ever.

Any words I tried to utter became ineffable, and I held back tears. I was elated that someone like Oprah had believed in the product. I never doubted my capabilities, not once. Although my entrance into the world of makeup artistry wasn't the smoothest and easy-going, I never dwelled on my past mistakes and inefficiencies, carried an excellent mindset, and was ever-determined to hone my skills and perfect my craft.

This fleeting moment lingered in my mind for minutes. Me, Khuraira, has created a product that Oprah found worthy of using. I could not wait for the phone call to end so I could call my husband, assistant, and clients to share the great news. Since it was a phone order, we couldn't post anything about it, but I was delighted that my products somehow had made it to Oprah and that she appreciated them.

That was the highlight of the surprising things positive thinking brought my way. Believing in something, putting in the needed energy, and knowing that you have put that positive vibe out there is fulfilling even if it doesn't happen.

I have seen the greatness of positive reflection in the Oprah story and how my aunt Zainab thought my life would be better than it was; she thought of it and said it often. Always believe in yourself and have a positive attitude toward what you want in life. It teaches us that what you put out is what you will receive.

# KHURAIRA INVISIBLE POWDER

Normally, we wouldn't pitch products here, but the Khuraira Invisible Powder is the best product we've ever used for keeping the shine down on interviewees. It was recommended by a colleague who worked on Oprah's Next Chapter – apparently Oprah loved it. Anything that works for the big O is good enough for us. But seriously, it really looks great.

*Khuraira Cosmetic's Invisible Powder ordered by the Oprah show.*

Later, in 2012, I was doing an event in Lagos, Nigeria, when I got a call from my husband telling me what he had found when he googled Khuraira Cosmetics. We periodically used Google to see if we appeared in any blogs or notable press. He found a blog from a TV producer raving about the Khuraira Invisible Powder and how he was introduced to it by a Harpo Production producer. Immediately we shared the blog on social media; our invisible powder sold out at the event and online.

I am forever indebted to Oprah and her close associates. Not only did she help the ball start rolling and give me the needed momentum to foray into the cut-throat, critic-filled industry of makeup, but she also made me forget about the low expectations of Rugga Fulani women.

Cross-continental recognition and brand ownership were not in the cards for girls like me, who are thought to grow up to be, at most, domestics and chained to the demands of our spouses. My defiance of social conventions and constrictive castings of women in the economy got me where I am today.

Sometimes it's just not enough to work hard, especially when there are natural oppositional forces that work tirelessly to bind you to a life of endless misery. You must be keen enough to distinguish between just societal norms and unjust ones. I was fortunate enough to have that foresight into what would've been a dreadful life if I had been "normal" like everyone else.

Being an immigrant woman of color comes with many challenges in the prime business industries in the US. Getting a trademark takes a lot of money. Furthermore, given the disadvantages of being a minority and a person without any private funding from family at the beginning, climbing up the ladder is a strenuous task.

That said, to get the attention of clients or customers, you have to work even more challenging. You have to sell your ideas. If you create a brand, there must be a story behind it. My narrative was about the frustration of not getting the right colors or shades of foundation and concealers for women of color each time I did make up for them including myself.

Committed to getting a solution, I looked for a way out. That was how I came about the dark circle primer. It was a hit. I was thus motivated to create Khuraira Cosmetics as a cosmetics brand.

My beauty line started with the dark circle primer. The solution brought resonated with many women, especially women of color. I always tell this story to anybody who cares to listen. As a makeup artist, whatever you produce has a story behind its production. Put another way, to show credibility for what you have created; you must prove your inspiration, beginning, process, and outcome. All of that can be captured in a story. So, I repeatedly tell the story of my dark circle primer as the demand for it arises.

*Khuraira Dark Circle Complex Primer*

When I launched Khuraira Cosmetics, I pitched my take-off product, the dark circle primer, to magazine editors, TV stations, and online stores. Its brilliance brought the attention we needed. Unfortunately, not everybody celebrates your success. My experience with an online beauty store comes to mind.

It is widely known for its collection of unique beauty products and typically sends samples of these products to its members in a box. If the members like them, they buy from the online beauty store, which gets your brand on their platform. My opportunity to pitch for this platform came after my late business executive, Jill, pitched it to a friend who worked at Elle magazine and referred her to the beauty buyer of the online store. After the pitch, she sent the sample of the dark circle primer to the buyer, who had terrible dark circles. It worked for her. She also loved the story behind it.

After that, the online beauty store tried to work with us to supply my dark circle primer samples. Unfortunately, we could not fill in the order because they wanted us to give them about 25,000 pieces, and Khuraira cosmetics had to fund them. We could not do so because, at the time, my son was in the hospital. He was battling his worst ever sickle cell crisis. We were not even sure if he was going to make it. Things were not going well for us.

So, my foremost priority at that time was my son's health. We kept going back and forth with the online beauty store, until eventually, the communication stopped. I have every email exchange to prove this. I didn't think much of it again because my son's health was the most important thing at that time. After Hanif survived the crisis and was okay, I tried to revisit the discussion.

On January 16th, 2016, I contacted the beauty buyer assigned to my account, but her response was quite cold. Little did I know that their beauty buyer, who had terrible dark circles, had used my story of using Orange-red lipstick on a YouTube video to show how to eradicate dark circles.

She took our intellectual property by knowingly using the idea we shared with them when pitching the product. She leveraged the online store fan base to promote the video helping it to go viral. She also used TikTok and Instagram to tell the same story. Moreover, she was invited to major TV networks to share her brilliant idea of using Orange-red lipstick to cover dark circles.

Boldly and confidently, she said my account and claimed it as hers. Overnight she became a sensation which opened doors for her to get investors to fund her beauty brand.

I'm highly disappointed that the online store will betray our trust. We believed they would protect whatever information we shared with them during our negotiation. Allowing one of their beauty buyers to do such a thing under their watch shows serious negligence.

What happened to me often occurs between big bucks corporations and upcoming brands with limited capital. With the benefit of hindsight, I often advise makeup artists or small business owners to keep records of every conversation they have with any buyer or business in case something like this ever happens.

Whatever you can do to protect yourself, do it. I have not given up on the issue yet: I want to challenge the beauty buyer now brand owner someday. I would like her to discuss how she came up with the Orange-red lipstick idea.

I hope and pray that we meet so she can face her audience for her to tell them how she came about the idea of neutralizing the dark circles using the Orange-Red lipstick. Intellectual property theft is a massive crime in the business world. How she discovered the secret of using orange-red lipstick to neutralize the blue will be very interesting to hear from her. Let her be honest and say it. I pray for the opportunity for us to be on the same stage to discuss it.

My issue with that buyer is one of the many challenges I have faced in growing my business and building my career as a makeup artist. Nevertheless, I draw a lot of strength from my faith in God and destiny. I believe that whatever is destined for me will surely come my way.

On the other hand, my highly soft spot for people has not helped me. It is a weakness: I easily trust people. Often, it lands me in something I never saw coming. I have lost money in the business as a result of this. On the other hand, I have also learned a lot from this Achilles heel. I am still learning how to manage it. It all comes from my compassion for the world.

Becoming a female entrepreneur is one of the wisest choices I have ever made for myself. One cannot stress the importance of financial independence for a woman in this day and age. I remember, after my second marriage ended, I promised myself that I would never be solely financially dependent on anyone. I vowed to work as hard as possible to provide for myself, my children, and my extended family as it became evident that I would need to learn to fend for myself.

I believe that all of us have unique God-given talents. Our lives are inherently limited as African women because our culture portrays us as subordinate to men. As our lives progress without foundation, we often regress when facing adversity.

There may come a point in a marriage when love is lost, divorce happens, or even death occurs. Regardless of these outcomes, financial independence is imperative. After the sudden death of my late husband, I had to face the music of widowhood. There were no more phone calls, no one else to keep an eye on the kids, and no one to provide for them. Being in a similar position twenty-eight years ago, it was evident that I had to step up and fulfill both parental roles. Although I was my family's only source of income, my children did not need to work to survive. They were free to continue their childhood and focus on their education.

Putting all of your fate in the hands of your partner is risky. Don't sit back and ignorantly believe that everything will work out because of a higher power. Regardless of one's constant manifestations and prayers, one must be willing to help themselves and persevere.

A Promised Land

"You may not always have a comfortable life, and you will not always be able to solve all of the world's problems at once. But don't ever underestimate the importance you can have because history has shown us that courage can be contagious and hope can take on a life of its own."

Michelle Obama

## When the Chips are Down

*The gem cannot be polished without friction, nor man perfected without trials."*

Chinese Proverb

Some of the most significant challenges of my life have come in my family life. Herein, I am grateful to have seen the miracles of God pulling us out more robust than ever before.

When my second marriage ended, I remarried and had three sons: Jamil, Kamil, and Hanif. When I was pregnant with Jamil and Kamil, I had an amniocentesis test to check for abnormalities. My husband was tested for his genotype since I had the sickle cell trait. After the examination, he was found to have the trait too.

We went through counseling to educate and prepare ourselves before the boys were born. Since we both have the trait, we were told there is a 25% chance one of our children will inherit the disease. We were devastated and kept praying for the remainder of my pregnancy.

When I finally had the twins, they both didn't have the SS genotype, which causes the disease. We were relieved. Two years later, I had Hanif. We assumed Hanif would be okay too. Unfortunately, when the state sent the results of neonatal blood taken during his birth, we got the shocking news that our baby boy had an SS genotype. Our doctor instructed us to take him to the sickle cell center for evaluation. The information shattered us.

I thought I would die that day. I cried my eyes out. Much later, when I was a bit calm, I researched sickle cell anemia, just about when we began frequenting the sickle cell center to be oriented on his health.

I was tired of the whole situation, and the doctors drove me crazy with all the bad things that could go wrong. I didn't want to hear such information anymore and convinced my husband for us to stop going. I knew people with sickle cell anemia in Nigeria who didn't have to go through counseling; they got the crisis and turned out okay, and I thought the same would be for Hanif. I even doubted the doctors that Hanif was SS because Hanif was fine for six months and never got sick.

We did not know that the neonatal blood in his system kept him crisis-free. Immediately after the six months, the crisis started. Almost every month, he had to be hospitalized due to severe pain. The worst crisis happened when he was eight years old.

I remember him telling me that he had some pain in his back. I looked at his father, and we both knew the crisis was about to start. Each time he complained about pain in the joints or back, it was a sign that things were about to worsen. He was in excruciating pain that night; he stayed awake screaming his lungs out due to the severe pain until the doctor recommended, we give him a little morphine, which helped him sleep.

As a makeup artist, sometimes, I had early morning makeup appointments for people who had TV interviews or Bar/Bat mitzvahs. Making it to those appointments with Hanif's condition was tough. The night of the crisis in question was a Friday. The following day I had an appointment. I left early while my husband stayed with Hanif. Later in the day, he called to say Hanif was getting worse.

"Get an ambulance," I replied sharply, given the urgency of the call. Hanif was thus taken to the nearest hospital. Less than 24 hours after his complaint, he was admitted.

Kamil, Jamil, and I joined them later. Hanif was having problems with his lungs and couldn't breathe. If his condition didn't improve, the doctor said they would recommend a better-equipped hospital for his condition.

However, they would keep an eye on him until the morning. Relieved, I took the twins home while my husband stayed with our Hanif.

Barely two hours until our return home around midnight, he called. He told me that Hanif's condition had worsened, and he would be moved to another hospital. He was hysterical that I couldn't even make up what he said. I quickly got Kamil and Jamil, who were already sleeping, ready. I arrived at the hospital right when the ambulance arrived to transport Hanif to Maria Fareri Children's Hospital in Valhalla, NY. As soon as I entered the ambulance, I went to Hanif's side at the speed of lightning. I held his hand and prayed, "God, please, don't take my son."

I kept the faith, my heart racing with anxiety and fear throughout the ride. When we got to the hospital, it was lit up with doctors and nurses awaiting Hanif's arrival. Hanif was put on a ventilator and some indescribable equipment. My little boy was wired to four to five different machines. They did dialysis to stabilize his condition, and soon enough, it began to look like things were starting to improve.

The head doctor sought to speak with us privately while other doctors and nurses observed Hanif. We asked our twin boys to wait in the hospital kitchen so we could have some time with the head doctor.

"We are carefully monitoring your son and doing our best to save his life," the doctor began, "Your son is very sick based on our examinations. We will do our best to save him."

Not long after this sad news, my husband had to go home with the twins. Hanif was not responding well to the treatment. He was getting worse. Usually, in the ICU, they ring bells loudly to announce that someone is not responding to treatment or dying. Suddenly, I heard the loud sound of bells ringing. It was Hanif! One of the doctors said, "You need to sign this, permitting us to place Hanif in a medically-induced coma."

I could sense the urgency as the doctor placed the paper in front of me to sign. I was confused and scared. I honestly didn't know what it meant and was afraid to commit without my husband's consent. "You can call your husband if you wish, but it has to be done asap to save him," the doctor added.

I knew I couldn't call him. He had high blood pressure. The shock of the worsening condition could break him down in inconceivable ways. I had to sign the form, tears flooding my cheeks; I signed on the dotted line while begging the doctor to ensure my son didn't die.

It was a terrifying moment. We prayed and prayed. I asked God to at least keep Hanif alive; if not for my husband and me, then for the twins. They were constantly praying and believing that God would heal their baby brother. After saying this prayer, I felt a surge of warmth enveloping my body. I believed that God had answered my prayers.

Six weeks after the induced coma, it was time to wake Hanif up. When he was awake, he was not himself. The doctors said he had been in an induced coma longer than he should have been. They fear the possibility that his brain might have been affected, as he didn't recognize us. He couldn't talk, eat or sit. He had to be taught everything from scratch.

I researched how to make people who have been in a coma respond quickly. I discovered that allowing him to play with my iPad will help him remember something. He naturally liked my iPad. Therefore, luckily, it worked, and Hanif started responding.

Would you want to see your friend, Jeremiah? I asked.

He then smiled, which was a good clue! Immediately, I called Jeremiah's parents. I begged them to bring Jeremiah. Luckily, they accepted my request. They brought Jeremiah to meet us at the hospital's ICU, where we had been for months. Hanif was so happy when he saw his friend. That was the day he started improving, after two whole months.

A few days after his friend's visit, I returned home to check on its condition. We had left home to stay by Hanif at a residence provided by the Ron MacDonald Foundation. While still in the house, a call came in from my husband, who was with Hanif. I picked up the phone to answer the call. I heard Hanif's voice on the other end. He said, "Mommy."

I was so excited that I fell off the stairs. I drove with a sprained leg, blood gushing from the back of my head from the fall, to get to my son. But I couldn't see him right away because my husband suggested I go to the emergency to be checked. I checked into the emergency room, got my head stitched, and treated my sprained leg. I was hurting bad, but all I could think about was hugging my Nif and hearing him say the word Mommy again. I was happy my son was recovering and was talking. It was a good thing. I thanked God for healing him.

Dr. Mitchell Cairo I chief of Pediatric Hematology, Oncology, and Stem Cell Transplant and the Children and Adolescent Cancer and Blood Diseases Center director at Maria Fareri Children's Hospital at Westchester Medical Center. He told us that Hanif was not completely out of danger. However, I was pretty pleased with the miracle of his speech recovery, as it was a big step.

At this point, Hanif had two options: either he got a bone marrow transplant, or we let him be, but if he suffered other lungs attack, it would not be guaranteed he would survive because his lungs were severely affected by Respiratory Distress Syndrome (ARDS) caused by the sickle cell disease.

He had about an eighty percent chance of being cured with the transplant. Dr. Cairo, a researcher, and a practicing physician, also had terrific success in bone marrow transplants. We had a family meeting and discussed it intensively. We took option one to save him. Two of his brothers, Kamil and Jamil, were tested, but none matched.

Then, Dr. Cairo recommended we use the parents as the donors through a new experimental treatment that was newly introduced called the half-matched. A mother is safer because the child has already been in the mother's womb for nine months, and the genes recognize each other. The rejection rate is low in this method. So, Dr. Cairo opted for me. The procedure was to implant my cells from my bone marrow into his own body.

We agreed, and I had to take a Neupogen injection to help create more white blood cells. The side effects were excruciating pains in my bones, but for my baby to survive, I was okay with it. I took the treatment for a week. Then they performed minor surgery to collect the blood. Next was to kill all of Hanif's old cells to prepare him for the transplant. Hanif had just started the treatment to kill his old cells, and his father got the news which shook us to our core.

My husband was getting Hanif's medication at the pharmacy when he met a woman who told him her daughter had gotten similar surgery, but it was fruitless. My husband came back with noticeable emotion and told me the story. I immediately called one of the doctors to tell her that we wanted to rethink doing the transplant. I feared Hanif wouldn't make it.

"Well, Mrs. Mouehla, it's not possible because Hanif has already started the transplant process. She calmed me down, saying, "Don't worry; our priority is to help save lives." Upon hearing that, I felt confident that Hanif was in excellent hands under Dr. Cairo's and his team's care.

I trusted them against all visible odds. Thanks to God, it finally worked out well. Our boy made it! Hanif is now sickle cell disease-free and an advocate for sickle cell treatment. He has helped champion the idea of half-matched bone marrow transplants and through his advocacy many are living a healthy life as him.

*Hanif's journey.*

Although it seemed like the clouds started to clear and the sun began to show its face, another tragedy struck my family. On midnight, April 5th, 2020, my husband unexpectedly suffered a ruptured brain aneurysm. Although the family was familiar with his plethora of health issues, we weren't used to this sight: him lying supine on the floor, making indistinctive noises. Anger, sadness, and utter confusion could be seen on our faces.

Luckily, one of my sons had already called for an ambulance to arrive and resuscitate him. For six minutes of silenced madness, we sat there waiting for the sound of an ambulance siren. Alas, they arrived, and the vehicle operators came bolting towards our door. They marched upstairs and began their standard medical procedures when dealing with an unconscious individual. As they performed the mutually stress-inducing operation, I was downstairs with a fraction of my children, grabbing onto them for comfort and assurance that everything would be okay.

Although my boys appeared confident that their dad would make it, I knew they were just as scared of the evitable outcome of death as I. I assured them their dad would be okay but would be transported to a nearby hospital, where they would adequately check the magnitude of his condition. I could only think of the worst, especially with the current state of his health. I spent the night with him, praying for some miracle and just one glimpse of life.

After hours of persistent prayer, I got tragic news: "Your husband isn't going to make it." said the doctor. "He has suffered a ruptured brain aneurysm, and there is no brain activity in his current state."

I fell to the floor in angst. The doctor's words echoed in my head for minutes, and I was in disbelief. I implored her to retest for any signs of activity in his nervous system, but they said they tried everything they could and any other effort would bear no fruit. Brokenhearted, I sat in my car thinking about how I could break the devastating news to our boys. It was the hardest thing I had to do. I drove home to deliver the unfortunate news to my kids. Immediately I stepped into the house before I could even say a word, the kids knew what was bound to come out of my mouth, and

I saw an unseen outburst of emotion from all of them. Life had taken a turn for the worst. Five years after Hanif got a new life, his father was suddenly taken away from us.

The year 2020 was the most challenging year for me. After losing my husband and experiencing an all-time low in my business, I had come into 2021 hoping to rise a bit. Then suddenly, the COVID-19 pandemic got worse. I got coronavirus in 2021, right before the widespread dissemination of the vaccine.

I thought it was terrible flu because my flu cases are usually awful. While on the phone with my friend Suleiman, he asked me to check my oxygen level with the pulse Oximeter he recommended for me to get earlier. The result of my oxygen level was 82%. He urged me to leave immediately for the hospital.

Kamil, one of the twins quickly rushed me to the nearest emergency. In just a matter of minutes, I was disoriented and could barely stand. I was gasping for air, which was so scary. Immediately after we arrived at the emergency, the nurses rushed me to a room to be given oxygen and tested for Covid. The results confirmed I had Covid.

I was hospitalized for six days due to my erratic temperature, which concerned the doctors and nurses.

After three days of trying to stabilize me, the doctor suggested I receive Plasma from Covid19 survivors to help me. I didn't argue, and I wanted to live for my kids. All I was thinking of was fighting to survive. My boys had just lost their father and prayed to God almighty not to take mine. I was petrified of losing my life and not being around to see my boys go to college and reach adulthood.

Barely able to talk, I gave my friend, Hope, a call to promise me if I didn't pull through, all my boys would get to go to the college of their choice. Before I got Covid, she was helping me with Jamil and Kamil's college application process. She had done it with her kids, who graduated from Harvard and Sarah Lawrence University, and knew she would help the boys.

The nurses were terrific, taking turns to check on me. They encouraged me to fight, not to be afraid. "Covid likes it when you get scared and stop fighting," one of the nurses told me. I can't talk enough about how much these nurses helped. Only God Almighty can reward the health care workers who cared for Covid patients.

Laying on the hospital bed fighting for my life got me thinking. If I die from Covid, my young children will never get to know who their mother was. Her struggles before having them. The fear of losing my life made me determined to write my memoir.

After all of this, I went back to the brand. It revived and focused on a different concept to expand it. Things were good before COVID hit. Then suddenly, we were forced to close our store which we had for over 15 years. We have refocused on our online business and working with a business strategist, and things have finally started looking promising.

For the first time in my life, I had seen myself tremble and was genuinely lost on how to continue running a business when it seemed like all the odds were stacked against me. This pandemic was unforgiving, as I saw a tear-jerking plunge in my customer base and a sharp decline in productivity. Phone calls from customers stopped coming in, and I questioned my competence as a makeup artist.

"Was I good enough to stay in this industry?"

I repeatedly thought to myself. Self-doubt and sleepless nights, brought upon by constant catastrophizing about possible critics, haunted me for weeks. I almost dropped the makeup brush and made my exit from the industry.

Despite my low self-confidence, I still felt like I needed to keep going for my kids, my late husband, and those who had believed in me when such belief was perceived as foolish and laughable. The young Fulani girl, who had been kicked out of her home and dreamt of being independent, would disapprove of my quitting.

Although I have come so far, I have many visions for the elevation of this business, and resigning this early, what good would that do for me?

I came so far, defying expectations and changing the cultural paradigm for young, unsung girls like me. Instead of heading toward the exit sign, I experimented with modernizing Khuraira Cosmetics to appeal to a younger demographic market. I became ever-receptive to new ideas to expand and broaden my business offerings

We have come up with a different concept of setting up satellite locations in high-end bridal and event boutiques, salons, and spas. I have always envisioned having a makeup brand that supports and uplifts local makeup artists and minority communities who do not have the funding to start their makeup businesses. As such we have created an affiliate program to help sell our products with no investment.

All they need is to place a Khuraira Cosmetics affiliate link on their social media pages or website to start earning income. The commission starts from 20-40%.

Also, with the rollout of Khuraira DIY customized airbrush foundation coming out in the fall, the future is looking very bright for our brand.

Define success all you want – from where I hail from to what I have accomplished, I feel blessed to have achieved some success. I'm still standing, unscathed' and I'm ready to wreak more havoc in this world that is not comfortable with the success of a fearless, unapologetic Black woman.

## Giving Back to Humanity

"No one has ever become poor by giving."

Anne Frank

I began my foray into charity long before I even knew what charity was. Thanks again, to Aunt Zainab, for unconsciously instilling that in me. I watched her consistently using her money to help those in need early in my life. She wasn't wealthy but always wanted to share whatever she had.

"What you give, she would always say, is what you have when you leave this world... not what you have stored in your house or bank account. Doing that brings you so much happiness and peace, especially when you do it expecting nothing in return!"

That was quite a lesson. Aunt Zainab didn't believe in hoarding as much as she could for herself to the detriment of others. She spent and would be spent for the good of others. She went the extra mile to put a smile on people's faces she knew nothing about, except that they needed her. In hindsight, one could say that the sudden possibility of finding a blood donor for me when my survival hung on it was one of the rewards of her kindness to humanity.

My father also symbolizes that for me. He was a very generous man. He was always kind to people, those he knew and those he didn't know. He generously shared what he had with others. It was so typical for him

I grew up knowing that you always have to give to help others. To Aunt Zainab and my dad, I owe the foundation of my eventual commitment to charity.

Currently, I am involved with a lot of initiatives. I founded some and am just an active participant in others, lending my help financially or through mentorship, whichever angle I feel comfortable.

I am involved with breast cancer campaigns, reaching out to survivors and patients. Through Khuraira Cosmetics, I speak to these women in dire need of treatment to survive. It is one of my ways of giving back to society.

The concern for breast cancer patients was born through an encounter with one of my clients. The incident happened at the time I was about to open my store. A few weeks prior, another great client referred a lady to me. Within two months, that referral was canceled multiple times, booked several times, then canceled a day or two before.

That was getting on my nerves, but I kept calm for a while. Unfortunately, the situation did not change. Now, at that point, I knew I couldn't take it any further. I had decided never to give the client another appointment if she called again.

A couple of days went by, and she called. "I need to get my portrait done, and it is important I get it done today," she said. The finality with which she said it was different from all the other times. I remember it was on a Monday. I didn't open on Mondays. Worse still, the store was not officially open for business.

Well, I began. "We are not even officially open, but I will open the door for you and do your makeup. But, please, this time around, do not cancel on me.

"I promise you. I will not cancel on you. I will be there," Leslie replied quickly, stopping me from changing my mind.

An elegant, tall, gorgeous lady walked into my store a moment later. She was awe-strikingly radiant, as though in a beauty contest with the midday sun. She was full of smiles and apologies for all the times she canceled on me.

"I'm so sorry for all the cancellations, but finally, I have made it, she said."

I did her makeup. She looked more stunning than she already was. She told me about going to a photo studio to get a professional portrait of herself. A couple of weeks following that great session, the client who had referred her to me called to tell me that she had passed away." What!?" I screamed, shocked by the sad news.

"Yes, she has passed away, my client continued. "You know, the consistent cancellations of her appointment were not entirely her fault. She had cancer. She was going through chemo and was always too weak to come and see you."

I was shattered beyond words. Leslie's portrait, to date, hangs on the wall of Englewood Hospital, New Jersey, in a hall named after her. I haven't gotten the courage to go and see that portrait, but some of my clients always rave to me about it. She was a very well-known figure.

Leslie Simon is the reason I am involved in supporting breast cancer patients. I do fundraising activities for breast cancer organizations whenever asked. I am very committed to the campaign.

Next to that is sickle cell anemia. I am a spokesperson and an advocate for those suffering from the disease because of Hanif. I remember how I cried and prayed to God Almighty to help my son survive. Because of the peace of mind, I enjoy him being free of this terrible illness. I will support families in the same predicament; thank God for saving my son. It is the least I can do.

*Zainab Memorial School Pupils, with picture of kids before they enrolled in the school.*

Furthermore, I founded a primary school called Zainab Memorial School to give back to the community in which I had my earliest life. It was launched in 2013 and named after Aunt Zainab to honor her for her sacrifices in ensuring other kids, and I got an education.

I remember times I would send her money, and she would need more money the next minute. "Oh, God! What did you do with the money I sent?" I would ask, surprised that it had been spent so quickly.

Aunt Zainab's response was always about some child from one village or house who needed books, pencils, school uniform or shoes, etc., to go to school. She couldn't bear the suffering of others when she could do something about it.

She always told me not to get mad at her. She had lent a helping hand. Even at that, I pretended as though I was furious, but I would eventually send her more money. Whatever money I gave her, she immediately spent it in an attempt to help some child to go to school.

The school was established with 22 kids in 2013 and, as of 2022, has an enrollment of 175. We have, to date, graduated at least three classes. Some of our pupils are now in High School doing very well, while others have finished and married.

In the future, I would like to add vocational skills training to the curriculum, especially for young girls, who may get married immediately after primary school education due to tradition and religious beliefs. I want them to get some skills to generate an income to continue caring for themselves and their families.

*Children at the Zainab Memorial School.*

I had made a deal with the parents that no girl should be denied education even if she gets married before completing her primary school. It is usual for girls to start school late and reach the married age of 14yrs or 15yrs in some cultures, especially in Fulani culture. To allow them to continue their education agreement is reached between her parent and the spouse's parent with our school for their education not to be interrupted even if she is married and pregnant.

Through Zainab Memorial School, I am happy that I'm supporting the kids in the village. It doesn't matter the community they hail from, their religion, or tribe. As long as they cannot afford to pay for school, they are enrolled here for free. They don't pay anything except for a registration fee, which is minimal for unforeseen expenses and only applies to those who can afford it. Khuraira Cosmetics supports the school's maintenance and teachers' payments through proceeds of our sales of products and services.

In addition, as I explored my home country of Nigeria, I noticed the unfortunate plight of the youths, devoid of the requisite qualifications for employment and productivity. That concern led to the establishment of the Arewa Development Support Initiative (ADSI). The initiative is about empowering young men and women in Skills Acquisition. To be skilled helps to be financially independent. In northern Nigeria, men and women often finish school and wait on the government to give them non-existent jobs.

*ADSI Founding Members.*

Learning from the private sector here in the USA, I thought we could do something for my brothers and sisters back home. I noticed that most employment here comes from service-oriented businesses with skilled professionals for all kinds of jobs.

I took that concept and partnered with like-minded people to actualize it. We collect monthly donations, a minimum of 2,000 Naira, which is about $4, and no maximum limit, to empower young men and women with skills across the 19 states of northern Nigeria, including the Federal Capital Territory (FCT) of Abuja.

We have trained over 3,800 young men and women in different skills since its formation in 2019. It is heartwarming to know that some of them already have thriving businesses. We have also created a website with which, from 2022 onward, we will be fully functional for e-commerce. We plan to publish a list of all beneficiaries on the website and make their products or services available via the same platform, thus making it possible to sell anywhere.

Online presence also becomes another source of revenue generation for ADSI. All businesses operating on ADSI's website will pay some money to ADSI for each sale generated from the platform. What is raised is further deployed into the training in skills acquisition programs for other young Northerners, thus closing the unemployment gap as much as possible.

Our monthly dues are judiciously and transparently spent. Every member knows the amount collected every month.

It is posted on the official WhatsApp platforms of the organization. Similarly, expenses are posted for members to see what funds were used. No one is a paid member except those running the organization. We are not paying them a total fee of what it would have costs to render such services. It is just a small amount to oil the wheels of necessary operations.

ADSI is now evolving into a brand that can compete with the most effective charity organizations in the world. We have learned that a community can help itself without significantly depending on the government.

Aunt Zainab was right: What you give to others without expecting anything in return is what is genuinely yours. The joy you get is priceless. Giving back would make you happy and whole. What matters is the smile we bring to their faces during their dire needs without expectations, the sacrifice we make for those who can never afford to pay us back, and the commitment we make to better their lives that sum up the heartbeat of humanity.

# Chapter 5: The Amazonian Women

"I wish more women realized that helping another woman win, cheering her on, praying for her, or sharing a resource with her, does *not* take away from the blessings coming to them. In fact, the more you give, the more you receive. Empowering women doesn't come from selfishness but rather from selflessness."

Selene Kinder

There is a saying that behind any successful woman are all other strong and accomplished women rooting and cheering for her. This saying is profoundly well suited to my life.

This chapter is dedicated to some of the amazing women in my life that I have had the honor to meet and call my friends and incredible supporters, who have encouraged me, cheered me on, challenged me, and supported me in building my brand. These women are faithful supporters of Khuraira Cosmetics and my charitable organizations who played significant roles in developing my brand into what it is today.

Dear ladies, I turned into the independent and empowered woman I am today because of you and your impact on my life. I appreciate these fascinating, talented, and selfless women for being there for my brand. And that's solely why I am here, dedicating a chapter to all the powerful and awe-inspiring women who helped me become my light for guiding my way ahead.

First and foremost, I give my regards to **Hope E. Daley-Derry.** The remarkable woman is more than a friend; she's my dear friend who has been with me for more than eighteen years through thick and thin. We met in a beauty salon one day. I remember I had just given birth to my twins and was, at that time, working to build my beauty brand. We started talking about our plans, and the rest, as they say, is history.

Hope was the beacon of hope I had wanted in my life. We were there for each other, our children, sadness, and happiness. It was wonderful to see Hope flourishing in all of her roles. She taught me that a woman could excel in all the roles life demands from her. The secret ingredient is to keep your spirits high and not back away from challenges.

Often, when life felt overwhelming, I used to think of Hope. If she can handle being an entrepreneur, a corporate event planner, a writer, a wife, and a mother of two superstars, it means she's courageous and ambitious enough. That thought would inspire my soul and urge me to fight my obstacles and try, try and try again until I succeed. Life isn't a bed of roses, but you can undoubtedly pluck away the thorns with your fearless and overpowering determination.

Thank you, Hope, for teaching me this vital lesson. I think I connected with Hope because we had quite a few things in common. Although she was born in the States, her parents had migrated from Jamaica. In addition, we bonded over our joint ambition of women empowerment- not just for ourselves but for other women worldwide. helping struggling females through mentorship and encouragement- her not-for-profit organization is proof of her ideology of "giving back to society."

**Suzzanne Douglas** was an exceptional soul. She was a phenomenal actress and the epitome of creativity and enigmatic artistry. Oh. How I miss her dearly. Best known for her roles in Law and Order, Bones, and The Good Wives,Suzzanne left several-including me- in pain and tears when she passed away in 2021.

We met when I was working for Laura Mercier at one of their locations at Neiman Marcus. I saw someone hopping from one counter and another, searching for makeup. Immediately, I recognized her as one of my role models. I approached her and introduced myself. I'm a huge fan of hers and could not help but tell her how spectacular she was in her role in "Stella Got Her Groove Back." She smiled and thanked me. She was searching for a foundation that would not turn ashy after oxidation, one of the major issues women of color face with makeup.

I took her to three different brands, including the one I represented, to get different shades that I put together to create her perfect shade. She was blown away, and there our friendship started. She encouraged me to develop my makeup brand and was there to help me promote it.

She also advocated for Sickle Cell Disease and offered her time for it.

**Jodi Epstein** is a symbol of women's leadership. She's more than a wife, mother, and grandmother. She's also the glue for every business she works with and the community work she contributes to. Her accomplishments and philanthropic work have earned her an affectionate nickname of "rainmaker," which enthralls me. Her values, ethics, and philanthropy are outstanding, and there's no role Jodi cannot take on. She's one of the kindness women I have met, and I am proud to call her a friend.

Jodi is instrumental to my success in the Jewish community. She introduced me to affluent ladies. I was introduced to her by one gentleman who would connect designers with clients. Jodi asked if I could do her makeup, and she absolutely loved it when I did.

Because I was new, she told me she'd introduce me to the JCC to do a lavish lunch event. I remember how she advised me to be calm and do makeup for others as I did for her. She said, "They love you, and you're set in Tenafly." That was 18 years ago; since then, Jodi has been family to me. She's one of the most generous persons I've ever known, a supportive and kind woman who loves helping other women excel.

Next, I offer my gratitude to **Wendy Federman**. She's one of my oldest clients, and she taught me that a woman could just as well achieve her dreams while building the family life she craves for. Her life is a testament to her successful career, and as a friend and loyal client, I have first-hand experience witnessing her manage her work and personal life.

It astounded me how she kept a balance between her hobbies, corporate career, and family time. I learned from her the importance of self-care even when life feels like a tightly-packed schedule. Even when her job got challenging, Wendy never once compromised in her indulgence in the things that brought her happiness. More than this, I strengthened my beliefs about philanthropy the more I spent time with Wendy. Wendy further fueled my ambitions to do good for society.

Her guest lectures for charity foundations and mentoring programs for aspiring actors, writers, and producers made me, even more appreciate her existence in my life. Our relationship started when she was introduced to me by one of her friends seventeen years ago. It was just before she began her journey with the Broadway Production. Today, I'm in charge of her makeup for every occasion, from special family gatherings to her Tony Awards events. She continues to support my brand and the charitable organization greatly.

Thank you, **HajiyaAsabeBala Adamu**, for allowing me to know you and enabling me to feel motivated in my life. She is truly the most loving and generous woman I've ever met. Hajiya was introduced to me by a mutual friend when I first moved to Kaduna from Jos. I was her junior, but she instantly took me close as her little friend, guiding me through the meaning of surviving my new life surrounded by ladies married to prominent Northern Nigerian men.

Hajiya always encouraged my desire to establish my business and even helped me get acquainted with wholesalers selling home décor in London and gold and children's clothing in Saudi Arabia. Moreover, Hajiya also introduced me to shop owners, spas, and influential women who could buy from me.

After I launched Khuraira Cosmetics in Nigeria, she recommended I get the products sold in high-end boutiques and beauty spas. Hajiya even arranged my meeting with H.E. Aisha M. Buhari who owned thriving beauty spas before becoming Nigeria's First Lady. All in all, Yaya Asabe, as we fondly call her, is among those who love seeing other women prosper. Of all her philanthropic endeavors, I'm awe-inspired by her strong advocacy for Girl Child Education and Almajiri kids, offering them job assistance and other necessities they may require.

If there is one thing I have learned from **Tracie Erwin, AKA T.H.**, there is no other option in life but to do a good job and give something to others. T. H. taught me that accepting anything but your very best is not okay! No matter what you endeavor to do, give it everything you've got. Don't do something unless your whole heart is in it. T.H. has taught me all of this by example, too.

She is an entrepreneur and marketing leader and is currently the co-founder of exEXPERTS, a platform for divorced women to come together for the support and advice they need. It is inspiring to see how T.H. took something as difficult and painful as her divorce and created so much good. Part of the platform is the Podcast that brings on different female experts to talk about all matters related to divorce.

T.H. has never been one to put a half-hearted effort into something for as long as I have known her, and I know that she will continue to be a unique and dedicated woman who inspires everyone around her. We met when she was a representative of Suburban Mamma, which features local businesses. Later, when she joined 201 Magazine, she ran "Women for Women," a social event based on women empowerment.

She featured me in one of her events, and I remember being appreciative of her efforts. Since then, she has always reached out to me to be one of the contributors to her events. When I faced difficulties with my brand, T.H. was there to give a helping hand. She pitches me in for magazines and even helps with the fundraising for my school as much as she can.

It's astounding how some women are born to be leaders, models, and motivators. For me, that's the role played flawlessly by **H.E Dr Aisha M Buhari**, the wife of the current president of Nigeria. I met H.E. Dr Aisha Muhammadu Buhari when I was looking for a location to place Khuraira Cosmetics products in Abuja, Nigeria. She was introduced to me by my dearest mentor HajiyaAsabeBala Adamu, whose passion for seeing women empowered is unmatched.

HajiyaAsabe loves seeing women own their businesses and thrive. When she found out about my plans, she suggested I meet with H.E Dr Aisha. She is a trained cosmetologist and we share the same passion for beauty. It was years before her husband became the president. She owned luxurious spas in Kaduna and Abuja. After our meeting, she congratulated me and agreed to allocate space for our brand in Abuja Spa and introduced it to all her client base.

H.E. is very passionate about women's empowerment which can be seen in her work as the First Lady of Nigeria and non-profit organization she birthed, Future Assured Foundation which focuses on women and children addressing reproductive, maternal, new-born, child and adolescent health. Her endorsement of Khuraira cosmetics was terrific and helped to expand our base. I'm forever grateful to H.E Dr Aisha M Buhari and my mentor HajiyaAsabe for their support.

Senator **Binta Masi Garba** is the true definition of women's leadership. She's a politician, businesswoman, administrator, philanthropist, and gender equity advocate. Her advocacy activities and efforts to promote women's education and healthcare-especially for youth and rural women- are causes close to my heart. Seeing such a dynamic lady working to make a difference in women's lives, helping them live happier and fuller lives, is refreshing. We met at an event about empowering women in Houston, Texas.

I presented about how makeup is an outlet to help women have their independence in doing the application or selling products and how Khuraira is a place that offers opportunities to aspiring women. At the time, I didn't know that Binta was the senator from Nigeria, but later on, we talked- and clicked. She loved my idea and got my number to keep in touch.

Later, she even opened a Khuraira boutique in Nigeria to support my business and give a chance to the local women. Today, I look at Binta and wish to accomplish half as much as she has. Her ideology to make rural and underprivileged women acquire education and become independent is wholesome. She sacrifices her time and energy to help other women, which is admirable.

Growing up, I wish I had someone like Senator Binta G. Masi in my Fulani settlement who could help other females see the light. It is an incredible honor that I get to call this woman a friend and confidant.

**Debbie Satnick** heard about my work after my event for the Lavish Launch run by the JCC. After the event, the news about Khuraira airbrush makeup went viral among community socialites. She has been instantly fascinated by me doing her foundation with an airbrush. I have done her makeup and daughters for over eighteen years.

Debbie has become a great supporter of the Khuraira brand and charitable endeavors. I've seen her evolve from an event planner to an asset for her family business in real estate. And every time, she

120

has proven to be a great role model for other women, exemplarily dealing with the challenges of her career and her tasks as a mother.

Another of my supporters, **NavinaChhabria**, is a humble and artistic soul who brought vibrancy to my life with her playful, imaginative, and fun character. Her creativity is motivating, inspirational, and awe-worthy. Not only does she put all of her innovation into her career but in her personal life too. I am truly blessed to have Navina, my go-to person, for my branding needs.

It's slightly humorous now that I think back to how we connected. My late husband found her on Craigslist when he searched for a graphic designer. She had recently immigrated from India and was searching for relevant jobs. As soon as we met, we just clicked. Navina is an immensely patient person who did my catalog, website images, posters, and business cards perfectly. She's a great illustrator and even got a book deal for that. We have worked together for many years, and I owe her a lot.

I met **Doris Acosta** in 2005 when she found me on Writeup. She loved how the model I did makeup on looked and called me for an appointment. She loved my application techniques; since then, I have been in charge of all her makeup requirements. She buys my products, sends her family and friends to my boutique, and even supports Zainab Memorial School in Nigeria.

If there is one thing I have learned from Doris, life is about reinventing yourself. If you aren't happy with how things are going or think it is time to move on to bigger and better things, you must follow that feeling. You can't let anything get in the way of what you truly want in life, and it is never too late to realize that. I thank Doris every day for teaching me this valuable lesson.

**Devika Mahadevan** is simply the modest and humblest person I have ever made. She is a devoted wife and mother. She was amongst the first to patronize my boutique in Tenafly. We immediately clicked when she told me her brother lived in Lagos, Nigeria, before returning to India. She is always there to encourage and push me, to never back down.

I remember getting an offer to sell my products on ShopQ, a TV shopping network. The order was huge, and I had issues funding it. I was telling her my predicament, and before I could say another word, she told me to hold off for her to make a call. The rest is history. I am grateful and blessed to have a diehard supporter in her.

**Diane Seiden** is a devoted daughter, wife, mother, proud grandmother, and an exceptional and inspiring woman. Her Philanthropic works are commendable. Diane was among the first ladies in Tenafly to visit my boutique. She warmly welcomed me to the community and jokingly said, "It is about time Tenafly get some flavor."

Diane has been a staunch supporter of our brand. We have done all her events makeup, and she always does her seasonal makeup lessons to stock up on Khuraira cosmetics. Her husband's company oversees the SEO of a mega makeup brand where free products are sent to her every season, but she instead patronizes businesses in her community. Diane's utmost priority is to see the businesses in her community continue flourishing. To have such a person as a supporter and friend is priceless.

I met **Robin Miller** when I was holding a master makeup class for fortune 500 corporate women at Laura Mercier in Bergdorf Goodman, NY. Part of my job as a national makeup artist is that I used to do seminars for prominent women, and Robin was one of them. When I opened my makeup boutique in Tenafly, she came and introduced herself and welcomed me to the community. I've done her makeup several times, even for her daughter's and son's weddings.

Robin is a massive supporter of anything and everything Khuraira, and be it any event or launch, she's always there, cheering for my success.

Another woman whom I had the honor of meeting, befriending, and looking up to for inspiration is **Andrea Stassou**. She was a news anchor at CBS and was introduced to me by other people who've tried and loved my makeup. I've been doing her makeup during her days at CBS to date. And since then, she has grown from a client to quite a dear friend.

As I did her makeup, I would silently observe her resilience and passion as she dealt with people around her. I marveled at the thought of how well and eloquently she covered stories during her career. I respected that she strived to be a woman who shed light on the truth and created awareness in the general public about whatever's happening in the world.

Another thing that inspired me was Andrea's devotion to charity. Looking at how high she prioritized her charity works made my heart feel lighter because of the relief that, yes, people as selfless as her still exist and continue being role models for the rest of us. Andrea was there to make sure I was okay during my tragedies. Her generous heart is unmatched.

We formed an even tighter "sisterhood" when Andrea started working with her Greek community and national organizations to raise money for breast cancer. I remember being ecstatic and trying my best to support a cause so close to my heart through my work as a makeup artist and recruiting others to help the endeavor. Moreover, Andrea and her family are massive supporters of Zainab Memorial School, and I am truly thankful to God for our special relationship.

I met **Daniella Ashabian** through one of her friends. Daniella was the bridesmaid, and I was responsible for the bride's makeup application and other bridesmaids fifteen years ago. And since then,

I've done Daniella's makeup uncountable times. She's a significant supporter of my school in Nigeria and the Khuraira brand, always sending her family, friends, and other brides to make my business bloom.

Daniella has taught me a lot about balance in life. I have seen how she has balanced her devotion to her family, community, and music. Giving time to one of those things never led to neglecting the others. I hope I have done even half as good a job as Daniella in creating balance in my life.

I think back to what made me connect with **Amanda Jacobellis** so quickly and conclude it to be our mutual profession. I give credit for meeting her to my late husband. My client was attending the Grammys, so my husband and I were in L.A. because I had to do her makeup for the event. While in the state, my husband suggested we visit Beverly Hills or West Hollywood to get inspiration for my brand- he was a marketing genius!

Even though I was tired to my bones, we still went and came across this makeup boutique, Makeup Mandy. The place was extraordinarily chic and relatively quiet, maybe because it was a Sunday and most celebs were busy with the Grammys. We entered the boutique and saw a woman who looked slightly distanced. I hesitated in meeting her, but my husband encouraged me to say hello.

That lady was Amanda, and she was an absolute sweetheart. Almost every celebrity visits her boutique for makeup and eyelash extensions; today, she even has her brand for lash extensions. We showed her my product and requested that she put it in her boutique to reach her affluent clients. She agreed because she loved the packaging. That was back in 2009; I've been with her since then. Today, she's a compassionate supporter of my brand and has put it in the hands of several celebrities.

**Tashieka Brewer** is a masterpiece. She has always told the most exciting and compelling stories for as long as I have known her and brings a positive attitude everywhere she goes. Knowing her for as long as I have, I can confidently say that she is an amazing woman to be around and is a constant support to those around her.

Tashieka worked as a marketing and public relations consultant for my brand, Khuraira Cosmetics. She created the Pink Girls Run the World platform because we were determined to make our narrative around how we see the world. If I inspired her at all, she has inspired me tenfold. Tashieka is an impressive lady who knows her stuff and has a great relationship with many emerging brand owners. And that's how she got my product into the hands of many beauty editors. Working with her was an ecstatic journey.

**Tasha Turner** is another spectacular woman who strengthened my belief in human spirits and the significance of women's empowerment. She was a beauty editor for In-Style Wedding and Essence Magazine. I met her through Hope when I launched my Khuraira brand. I started working with her when she featured me in InStyle Wedding online blog and later in Essence Magazine for my dark circle primer as a must-have product for brides on their wedding day.

I owe Tasha my debut on international and national levels because other beauty bloggers started picking my product and discussing it in their content after featuring me in online beauty blog and Essence Magazine. I remember Tasha's expressions quite vividly as she said, "This is the best primer for dark circles. I love your packaging. It's very chic." All of Tasha's friends and family would say that she is never one to be discouraged or let hard times slow her down. She has been a wonderful friend to me and an inspiration. Tasha has taught me the value of hard work and dedication and that putting in the hours will get you to where you want to be in life.

To the one whose resilience, determination, strength, and power taught me the true courageousness of a woman, **Ann Arnold**, you are one of a kind! I still find aspirations in Ann because she always does whatever sets her mind to. Her ideology of helping the underprivileged study and her excellence in the jewelry industry is remarkable. Her work for breast cancer awareness and promoting ecological practices is marvelous. And her personality as a confident and bold woman striving to accomplish more every passing day is majestic.

I met Ann through Triple-Negative Breast Cancer, an organization we both support. She's one of their valuable members. She and her Dad wrote a book about Holocaust. She is a reservoir of knowledge. So, Ann also became my go-to person when I started compiling my book. She would guide me and offer me tips when I'd get stuck somewhere. She always comes to me for all of her makeup needs. I have done her and her daughter's makeup severally. Ann is an extraordinary supporter of my school in Nigeria.

From Ann, I have learned that even a small contribution to a worthy cause can make a big difference. Like Ann, I wish to give my time and energy to each great cause that I can. I do not have to feel restricted, or like I cannot make a difference. I am always thankful to have such an inspirational woman in my life.

Our husbands introduced **Clarisse B Fall** and me. We immediately realized that we'd got a lot in common; we both came from Africa and made our marks here, and we want to empower youth and women in our countries. She learned about my brand and immediately took an interest in introducing it to her friends who own their businesses in Cameroon and Senegal. Clarisse interns in several public schools, work for maternal child health awareness programs, and vividly contributes to immigration and referral services initiatives to support African migrants settling in New York and nearby areas.

This great woman taught me how a woman could become a bright light of hope for several women, helping them achieve freedom from discrimination and abuse. Clarisse's ideology and social work, especially for the African Hope Committee, is a testament to the awe-worthy positivity in this world. Her ambitious leadership skills encourage me to keep moving forward and that there's hope for betterment. It's comforting to know that women like Clarisse work as spokespeople for several underprivileged. It's an honor to have her in my life.

I can't describe the positive impact of **Tracey B Limbardo** on my life. It's astounding to see Tracy fulfill her responsibilities as a loyal wife, proud mom of two grown sons, and devoted friend. Her philanthropic mindset and volunteer work, especially during the pandemic, are embedded in my heart. She's an incredible, giving, and generous soul I met when others referred me to her. From then, I've done her makeup for all her special occasions.

Tracey's charm is in her selflessness and devotion. All of Tracy's hard work and effort come from her heart. She has so much love to give without ever asking for anything in return. She has always put others before herself, making her a brilliant inspiration.

**Jan Rushton** doesn't only create beautiful homes; this kind and dedicated soul assists people in developing their dream spaces in Southern California, NYC Metro, and Dallas. She has been in the real estate industry for more than two decades and is a vivid supporter of "Marriage Today."

Jan was introduced to me while looking for makeup for one of her events. Since then, Jan has been a loyal client and friend. She loves our products and turned her daughters and sister into Khuraira Cosmetic's dedicated customers. We will always have so much to talk about whenever she is in New Jersey, from our kids, business ideas, and real estate. Jan is a reservoir of knowledge that helps me as often as I need.

Have you ever met someone with whom you feel an instant bond? Such people are God-sent, and I thank God numerous times for having **Marisa Sallen Kochnover** in my life. She has an infectious energy and such a kind and empathetic nature.

These qualities make Marisa not just an excellent friend but so good at everything she does. Marisa was introduced to me by my other clients. She owns CycleBar, so I'm responsible for the makeup application of the brand's instructors for press images and catalogs. I even do Marisa's makeup for her special occasions and family events.

She immensely supports my business and brings her friends to build and expand my loyal clientele. There's a long list of her incredible achievements, including her licenses as a Les Mills Body Pump Instructor, Social Worker in New Jersey, and member of the National Association of Social Work (NASW) and Association of Play Therapy (APT). Her role in charity and helping society, regardless of their gender, is a feat that makes Marisa a true inspiration to me and everyone lucky enough to know her. Everyone needs an individual who acts as a breath of fresh air and rejuvenates our souls whenever in their company.

I wouldn't be the version of me I am today if I didn't meet **Lisa Cole**. One of the most important things that Lisa has taught me is that a woman can be an incredibly devoted mother, raise an exceptional child, and still excel in her career and help those around her. She has shown me how much it is possible to achieve and that a woman never has to choose between family and career.

I admire Lisa's advocacy for mental health and eating disorders. And what I respect even more is her role of being a dedicated single mother of an 11-year-old who holds her daughter as her highest priority. I can honestly say that Lisa is one of the most inspirational women I know. She has uplifted me and done her best to support and help me. She has also taught me a lot about balancing my life and how to embrace motherhood and family life alongside my career. I am forever thankful to have Lisa in my life.

Next, I thank **SagarNdiaye**. She's practically the little sister I never had and was introduced to me by our husbands. She is Fulani from Senegal, and I'm from Nigeria. Therefore, it's no surprise that the sparks and instant connection happened immediately. The Fulani tribe is among the largest, spread across West Africa, and all Fulanis experience instant unity the moment we meet each other.

Sagar was a tremendous help during the later years of my career when I juggled between work and taking care of my twins. She would often babysit them while I was at work. After establishing my brand, Sagar also encouraged her younger brother, Mamadou, to distribute Khuraira Cosmetic's products in France even though he was a software engineer and didn't know enough about makeup.

Sometimes, I'm stunned by Sagar's strength. She is battling sickle cell disease, yet it still doesn't limit her from having three beautiful children and putting herself through nursing school. She graduated with honors despite the language barrier as she received her early education in Senegal, French colonized country. Today, Sagar is my go-to friend-turned-sister whenever the going gets tough. She is a solid, loyal, and brilliant young woman.

Here's to another of my cheerleaders who helped tremendously with my brand. **Sandi Kline** is an inspiration in how she strives to ensure every woman's story is heard. Every woman has lived a unique experience and has something worthwhile to say. And Sandy has made it a mission to give women their voice back and help them speak their truths! I love how intensely she encourages women's empowerment and motivates ladies to let their voices be known to the rest of the world.

I couldn't be prouder of my friend for her service to women. She runs a podcast, and we were introduced to each other by people who knew us. They told Sandi about my story and suggested she feature in one of her shows eight years ago. Sandi invited me, became a loyal Khuraira client, and the rest, as they say, is history.

Reading this quote, "I'm obsessed with seeing women encourage, support, and empower other women. It's my favorite. We need more of it", describes **Fatima Shehu.** She doesn't just create the most delicious dishes through her catering business; Her expertise can be seen in the A Lists Nigerian Northern Families events she has catered. She has been a part of the hospitality industry for over two decades and is a vivid supporter of "Educating of the Almajaris (Islamic students). " She employs, feeds, and educates some Almajaris in her community through her catering business.

Fatima was introduced to me when her late husband, a friend of my ex-husband, courted her over two decades ago. She loves our products and turned her daughter, friends, and family members into Khuraira Cosmetic's unwavering fans and a walking advertisement for our brand.

She tells everyone about Khuraira Cosmetics wherever she goes. Fatima is always happy and supportive of women's empowerment. She shares other women's successes with such passion, which is refreshing.

**Haley Dinerman** has greatly impacted my life because of her inspirational way of living and thinking. She has devoted much of her time to helping her fellow women and increasing awareness about breast cancer. What intrigued me the most was her aim of studying and working hard to do something that impacts thousands of women. She is one of the most selfless women I have met, and I strive to be more like her.

Haley does a lot with Triple Negative Breast Cancer. She's now the CEO of the organization. I remember when Haley walked into my makeup Boutique with her friend, Nancy, whose Triple Negative Breast Cancer is founded in her honor. I did Nancy's makeup for the organization's first event before she passed away. It was heartbreaking to hear that Nancy was sick and had a few months left.

Whenever they need my assistance for the Triple Negative Breast Cancer, I'm always there because of my advocacy for the disease. Haley and I also have a special connection because we're both mothers of twins, making our friendship even more relatable.

Last but certainly not least, thank you, **Barrister Maryam D Umar**! She's a brilliant young lady with a golden heart. Maryam is the daughter of my close friend, Halima, and Col. Umar Dangiwa, Kaduna state's former Military governor. Her passion for beauty prompted her to become Khuraira Cosmetic's early supporter in Nigeria.

I believe her advocacy assisted my products in penetrating the right niche of affluent young fashionistas. The way this enthusiastic woman excels as a law practitioner, wife, mother, and philanthropist is outstanding. She and her friends even founded a project to offer school supplies and warm clothing during the harmattan period for children.

Currently, she's an active supporter of JDL (Water for Life Organization) and ADSI (Arewa Development Support Initiative). Maryam is also an energetic contributor at Badr Nabi Foundation, which offers food charity during Ramadan. The world certainly needs more women like her.

Even though I've mentioned a hand full of women above, it doesn't mean that others didn't affect my life or touch my heart. I believe that every woman I've ever met or known somehow cast their impact and helped me turn into the Khuraira I am now.

From the women, I see rushing to take their children to school in the morning to the working mothers wrapping up their meetings because their child is at home and it's getting late. I appreciate you all for existing and showing the world that women are strong-willed and courageous beings who can conquer it all.

# Epilogue: My Aunt Zainab

"Her absence is like the sky, spread over everything."

C.S. Lewis

*Khuraira and Aunt Zainab.*

The worst day of my life was the day I lost Aunt Zainab. The launch of Khuraira cosmetics in Nigeria was in March 2012. My aunt Zainab was there to witness it.

She was so pleased and proud of both of us. She told me, "See what I have been saying, not to bother what anyone says about you? Look at how you now have your brand with your name." She gave me a squeezed hug and continued, "So, this is ours; Allah is GREAT," with her hands lifted, looking up at the sky. First time I have heard Aunt Zainab boast about something.

I hugged her tightly and said, "Yes, my old lady, this is ours, and you are part of this journey. You believed in me before I believed in myself, you did it, and I'm so grateful and proud of you."

The launch was held in Lagos and was a success; I took the team and her to a Chinese restaurant in Victoria Island, Lagos. We ordered so much food that she felt was a total waste because we couldn't finish it. When she saw the money, I handed to the waiter after we finished, she asked me how much it was.

Hearing the amount, she was distraught. Hurairatu, how can you spend this kind of money for something we eat and shit out tomorrow? She asked whether I knew how many cows we could buy with the money or how many poor people could get help in our village. Aunt Zainab's major spending was always about helping others or making sure we got what we need to improve our lives. She hated waste or extravagant spending. She begged me to be frugal with my money. I assured her not to worry; I would not overspend, making her feel at ease.

A few days after our event in Lagos, we did another in Abuja, which also was a success. We sold out our Invisible powder, but we had other items that didn't do well. She watched us discuss how everyone wanted the invisible powder, then she advised us next time to bring a lot of it and less of those that didn't sell.

My aunt was not formally educated but was brilliant, so I don't embark on anything without asking for her guidance and blessings. She liked that, and she always steered me in the right direction.

After two weeks in Nigeria, which I spent with her, I returned to America. April 12th is a date I will forever hold onto like my last breath.

On that day, I received a phone call from Aunt Zainab. Unfortunately, I was with a client and couldn't speak for long. I asked if I should call her back, but she insisted she wanted to talk to me. I said okay; she quickly asked how I was doing because I was under the weather from jet lag. She teased me of being the old lady, not her, since I couldn't stand being tired, and she is vibrant with no fatigue. I agreed and laughed it off. She asked after my kid's well-being by their names, then my husband. She emphasized if Hanif was okay because of his Sickle Cell disease. I assured her that everyone was OK.

She then said, "Love You and Bye."

Before I could say a word, she hung up. I called her after my clients and couldn't get through to her. I remember calling on Friday and Saturday morning but still being unable to get a hold of her.

I finally reached out to her neighbor, who told me our mom was okay, but she hasn't stayed home much since her return from Abuja. She has been going to the different homes, checking on her neighbors, sharing food items, and asking them for forgiveness.

I laughed it off and just took it as her usual self. She was found on Sunday morning, having passed away after failing to wake up for her morning prayers.

Because of our time difference, it was midnight here. My daughter, Hadizah, called her brother Salim to break the news and asked him to ensure I didn't have my phone with me until the morning. He communicated that to my husband, who hid my phone.

I woke up Sunday morning rushing to get to the makeup show in NYC, where we were exhibiting for the first time. It was our debut show. I couldn't find my phone, and my husband kept telling me to take the day off since I complained I was tired. He assured me that the artists would take care of everything, but I insisted I must go but couldn't find my phone.

While I was arguing with him about staying home, Salim walked in and asked me to take a seat. The way he spoke to me made me feel something was wrong.

So, I asked him, "Salim, did Hadizah get into a car accident?" Everyone knows how I have been very concerned about her driving herself. He shook his head no, then I immediately questioned, "My mom is dead, right?" There was a second of silence, after which he ran and hugged me and mumbled, "Yes."

Something huge got out of my body. I wanted to die. Nothing mattered at that moment. My old lady had left me forever, and the last words I heard from her were, "Love you and Bye."

Being a person of faith, I am the most grateful that God gave me the chance to spend those special two weeks with her where we stayed together throughout the trip. I shared with her my plans about Khuraira cosmetics, and she kept saying, "I'm so proud of you, and you with your children will never lack."

It is the happiest I have ever seen her, so I'm grateful that I could share those weeks with her.

# The Road Ahead

*"You may not control all the events that happen to you, but you can decide not to be reduced by them."*

Maya Angelou

I believe the best chapter for our company- and our lives is still yet to come when COVID is finally over. There is a lot in store for Khuraira despite all these trials. All my five children are successful individuals; thank God Almighty for that.

*Khuraira with her five children*

Hadizah, my first child and daughter, is married to a great man named Deji, a Barrister at Law and an LLM degree holder, and through them, I'm blessed with two grandsons, Femi and Fayo. She is a communication major from Montclair State University who was instrumental in developing Khuraira Cosmetics and continues to contribute to date. Salim, my eldest son, is a civil engineer from New Jersey Institute of Technology (NJIT).

Kamil, one of my twin boys, is a computer science major at Amherst College. Jamil, my other twin, is a Bates College Economics major with Mathematics minor who plays collegiate football.

My youngest Hanif is a senior at Northern Valley Regional High School in Old Tappan. Overcoming and persevering through life-threatening challenges, he is a Class President, a straight A student with an ambition of becoming a Hematologist to help find cures for children suffering from hereditary diseases. I can wholeheartedly say my children are my proudest achievements.

Professionally, I think I'm growing every day. Even the havoc caused by Covid brought the best out of me. My business staggered for some time, but these turbulent times improved my resilience, determination, and stubborn streak to prevent me from drowning in these rough waters.

Today, I'm humbled and content looking at my business recover and flourish after the uncertainty of the pandemic. Khuraira Cosmetics is at a great place right now, and I believe my future expansion strategies will further add to my brand's development.

Of course, life – or business – isn't always a smooth sail. I may encounter obstacles as I develop Khuraira Cosmetics to reach higher milestones. But I'm a vivid believer that I'll make the best out of every trouble that stumbles my way with such an inspirational and amiable group of loved ones behind me. Through

God's blessings, the audacity of this African girl has assisted her so far. It's sure to continue guiding her in the times to come!

Life isn't perfect, and not everyone is born with a golden spoon in their mouth. Everyone faces challenges; sometimes, life can get darkest for the longest time. However, that's where your determination can do wonders to help you through such challenging times.

Life wasn't easy as an orphan girl growing up in a Fulani settlement. However, it wasn't bad either. I had my ups and downs and even had to fight a few arguments in between. It wouldn't have been possible without God entrusting me to Aunt Zainab, my second mom, who took me as her own after my birth mother passed away.

During my childhood and teenage years, I made friends and got my education- and exposure to understand that we, as girls, are allowed and very much able to dream big and make them come true. The secret ingredient to making it happen is our courageousness and driving our spirits high to turn our goals into reality.

However, let it be known that accomplishing your dreams isn't easy. It doesn't mean you wouldn't face hardships once you achieve your ambitions. In fact, life is a pattern of highs and lows.

I also want to add that I was blessed and lucky enough to achieve my dreams, which in part was due to the fact that I was able to move to America where opportunities are given to whoever dreams and works hard to achieve it. I found America offered me the opportunity to build myself and brand based on merit not just who I was born as. In my home country of Nigeria, I found that merit was not appreciated as such as it is in America. It is a harmful practice that holds many talented people back. If that were not the case, then I am sure many people would have had the opportunity to actualize their dreams.

Sometimes, dreams don't work out for you either. The key is standing straight, chin up, and spine rigid, as you deal with the downs with unmatched resilience and embrace ups with poised modesty.

And during your lives, never forget the importance of charity. Charity during your success is one thing, but giving to society even when facing hurdles is powerful. It will do wonders to alleviate your pains and offer you contentment that helps you peacefully sleep even when times are hard.

*Khuraira posing in front of her cosmetic products*

As I conclude my book, the life journey of an audacious African girl who dreamt and continues to accomplish, I hope to offer you solace. I don't claim to be a role model. But I want to present my life as proof that regardless of your ethnicity, religion, or social circumstances, every girl and woman is created to be a strong queen.

In the words of Michelle Obama, "There is no limit to what we, as women, can accomplish." Therefore, by the will of God, you have the power to face everything, so let your soul ignite the fire that fuels your ambitions to earn knowledge, acquire education, fulfill your goals, make a name for yourself, and maneuver through hardships successfully.

And as you proceed with your excellence, don't forget to appreciate and guide other women to reach their goals. After all, a female is the best support another female can have. **Remember, behind each successful woman is a group of other successful women who've got her back.**

# Reader Reviews

*"It's a work of dedication, aspirations, and courageousness I didn't know I had to read to uplift my spirits."*
**- Azubuike Odega**


*"I got chills as I read the author's loss of a mother. Truly a masterpiece!"*
**- Jimoh Amata**


*"Dear author, the world needs more women like you to become a safe and loving place where women can live freely!"*
**- Lisa Brown**


*"Mixture of tragic happenings and hopeful ambitions. What a story!"*
**- Adebayo Adekola**


*"A heartfelt story of a woman fighting demons and shaping a successful life for herself and her family. Hats off to your braveness, Ms. Musa!"*
**-Tiffany Cole**

# Bibliography

(n.d.). Retrieved from KhuairaCosmetics: https://khurairacosmetics.com/

(n.d.). Retrieved from Water for Life Charity: https://waterforlifecharity.org/

Dickens, C. (1859). *A Tale of Two Cities.* London: Chapman & Hall.

Dr. Dorcas Oluremi FAREO, W. A. (2020). *East African Scholars Journal of Psychology and Behavioural Sciences.*Kenya: East African Scholars Publisher.

*Fulani.* (n.d.). Retrieved from Britannica: https://www.britannica.com/topic/Fulani

Glasgow, K. (2018). *Girl In Pieces.* Ember.

Hackett, F. G. (1955, October). *The Diary of Anne Frank.*Cort Theatre, Manhattan, New York, USA.

*Home* . (n.d.). Retrieved from ADSI: https://adsi.org.ng/

Kenton, W. (2022, July). *Copyright Infringement.* Retrieved fromInvestopedia: https://www.investopedia.com/terms/c/copyright-infringement.asp#:~:text=Copyright%20infringement%20is%20the%20use,breached%20by%20a%20third%20party.

KUPFERSCHMIDT, K. (2020). Can plasma from COVID-19 survivors help save others? *Science.*

*Maternal Health.* (n.d.). Retrieved from United Nations Population Fund: https://www.unfpa.org/maternal-health#readmore-expand

Motherly. (2021, June 3). *You've got this, mama: 15 empowering quotes on giving birth.* Retrieved from Motherly: https://www.mother.ly/pregnancy/birth/youve-got-this-mama-13-empowering-quotes-on-giving-birth/

*Sickle Cell Disease (SCD).* (n.d.). Retrieved from Centers for Disease Control and Prevention: https://www.cdc.gov/ncbddd/sicklecell/index.html

Sparks, N. (1996). *The Notebook.* Warner Books.

*Triple-Negative Breast Cancer.* (n.d.). Retrieved from Centers for Disease Control and Prevention: https://www.cdc.gov/cancer/breast/triple-negative.htm

# Translated Terms

- Allah – God

- Fura da nono - Mix of Yogurt and Millet gruel.

- Almajiri - Islamic pupil scholar

- Rugga - Fulani Settlement

- Kunu - Pap or Porridge made of millet.

- Kasuwa - Market

- Bappa - Father in Fulani language.

- KununKanwa - Millet Porridge made with Potassium, native herbs, and millet powder

- Ruma - Mold

- Isha prayer- Night Prayer

- Sallah -Eid celebration

- Talle – An Orphan

- Quran - Quran

- Kuka - Soup made from boabab leaves

- Kubewa- Okra

Made in the USA
Columbia, SC
23 January 2023

3ab42ea7-1876-41f1-bfa7-e7a8332b5148R01